LT

PICK-UP
GAMES

PICK-UP
GAMES

The Rules, The Players, The Equipment

D.W. Crisfield

A MOUNTAIN LION BOOK

Facts On File
New York • Oxford

Pick-Up Games: The Rules, The Players, The Equipment

Facts On File, Inc. Facts On File Limited
460 Park Avenue South c/o Roundhouse Publishing Ltd.
New York NY 10016 P.O. Box 140
USA Oxford OX2 7SF
 United Kingdom

Library of Congress Cataloging-in-Publication Data
Crisfield, Deborah.
Pick-up games : the rules, the players, the equipment / D.W. Crisfield.
p. cm.
"A Mountain lion book."
Includes bibliographical references (p.) and index.
ISBN 0-8160-2700-5
1. Games—Rules—Juvenile literature. 2. Games—Equipment and
supplies—Juvenile literature. 3. Sports—Rules—Juvenile
literature. 4. Sports—Equipment and supplies—Juvenile literature.
[1. Games. 2. Sports.] I. Title.
GV1201.42.C75   1993
790.1'922—dc20 92-16296

A British CIP catalogue record for this book is available from the British Library.

Facts On File books are available at special discounts when purchased in bulk quantities for businesses, associations, institutions or sales promotions. Please contact our Special Sales Department in New York at 212/683-2244 (dial 800/322-8755 except in NY, AK or HI) or in Oxford at 865/728399.

Text design by Donna Sinisgalli
Jacket design by Steve Brower
Composition by Facts On File, Inc.
Manufactured by the Maple-Vail Book Manufacturing Group
Printed in the United States of America

10 9 8 7 6 5 4 3 2 1

To the Kid and the Dog,
my writing companions

CONTENTS

ACKNOWLEDGMENTS

I'd like to thank Jim Crisfield, Perry Crisfield, Saleh Dhaher, Louise Hurd, Emily LeVan, Mike Lowrie, Patt MacIntosh, Bill McClements, Susan McClements, Joe Mosso, Bob Mulroy, Doug Myers, Mike Portland, Sue Portland, Jim Scibetta, Floyd Short, Dave Titus, Don Ting, Carrie Wickenden, Linda Wickenden, James Wickenden, and Martha Wickenden.

INTRODUCTION

When I was 10 years old, my mother's favorite suggestion was: "Why don't you go outside and play"—which meant the television was turned off, the toys were left inside, and my friend Chris and I would sit on the porch steps and complain that there was nothing to do. Inevitably we'd wander around to the garage and get out the basketball to play a little one-on-one game in my driveway. Even though I was taller, Chris was a better dribbler, and I always lost.

Then one day my dad taught me a game called Horse, which was the answer to my prayers. It required no dribbling whatsoever, and Chris liked it too. The game called for any crazy shots we could think of, and nothing keeps a kid quite as entertained as silliness.

We played Horse for hours. As soon as we learned how to spell long words, we changed the name of the game to Hippopotamus, in order to make the game last longer. In time our skills improved and the shots got crazier. Somewhere along the way we learned a game called Around the World, which diverted our attention from Hippopotamus for a while. And then we invented Universe, a complicated, utterly unique cross between Around the World and Horse. I've described it in this book, but it may appeal only to two 10-year-olds learning the solar system in science class.

But Universe was our game, and it entertained us for years. When Chris moved to Minnesota, I tried to play it with other friends, but no one else had the passion for it that I did. I'll teach it to my children, though, and maybe it will catch on with them and their friends.

That's the history behind one pick-up game, but all of the games in this book were invented somewhere, probably by bored kids. These players most likely wanted to play the actual sport but were faced with an insufficient playing area, a lack of equipment or a shortage of players—so their imaginations kicked in. Horse and Around the World probably started in someone's driveway; Stickball and Stoopball were invented on neighborhood streets; and Keep Away most likely evolved on a playground during recess.

What exactly is a pick-up game? *Webster's Dictionary* doesn't define it, but in this book it's any informal game that is an offshoot of an established sport. By informal, we mean that the boundaries and rules are flexible and there are no referees. Players can adapt a pick-up game to suit their individual interests and skills.

Most pick-up games are easy to play. People are usually familiar with the base sport, so it's easy for them to catch on to the intent behind each game. The unique variations of these new games often cause them to spread quickly throughout the country and even across to other sports. You'll notice that a few of the pick-up games in this book are the same in different sports, and as a result it's sometimes hard to tell for which sport it was created first.

The base sports are listed alphabetically, but the games in each chapter are organized in a more developmental manner. Just as pick-up games have evolved from sports, so have pick-up games evolved from other pick-up games. Similar games are grouped together.

Many pick-up games also cross over from sport to sport. For cases in which the pick-up game is exactly the same in each sport (such as Bull in the Ring, which falls under basketball and field hockey), I have kept in the heads for "number of players," "equipment," and so on, but have cross-referenced the text to the earliest alphabetical entry to avoid redundancy. Other common pick-up games (such as Horse) have complete text for each, as the rules and setups vary from sport to sport.

In every sport listed here, it's possible to find at least one pick-up game that will suit you. If you want to play ice hockey but only have two players, the game of Icing is a good choice. If you have a volleyball but no net, then Nameball can be fun. And if eight of you go down to the tennis courts but find there is only one court available, then everyone can play Shuttle on that lone court.

Use your imagination. All of these games were made up somewhere; there's no reason why you can't make up one yourself. If you find your creativity is on vacation, just take one of these games and adapt it to your situation. If your backyard is too small for a game of croquet, then just wind the course around to the front yard. All of a sudden, you have a game of croquet that nobody else has invented.

I've tried to compile as many pick-up games as I could so they can be preserved and passed on to kids and gym instructors for a long time to come. The most popular games would have lasted without this book, but many more would have been left to die with the inventor. In fact, unless Chris created a small pocket of Universe fans in Minnesota, the game was as extinct as the dodo bird until this book came along.

I expect that kids will be the primary audience for *Pick-Up Games,* as they're the ones with the time and the desire to experiment with new games. But that doesn't mean that this book can't be great for adults as well. For instance, on days when he didn't have a scheduled game with the New York Giants, Willie Mays used to go back to Harlem and play Stickball with the neighborhood kids. Many regular folks play pick-up games too. Varmint Ball is a favorite Labor Day pastime among my friends, and I probably play the tennis pick-up game One on You more often than I play regular tennis.

This book also can be the perfect tool for coaches and gym teachers, especially when they are dealing with young children. The younger the children are, the harder it is to grab and maintain their attention. They don't want to practice skills, they just want to play. Most of the games in this book cover both bases. They are fun to play, yet the child learns a skill without knowing it. Even the silliest of games, like Balloonminton, can be helpful because the activity will familiarize children with the way their bodies work and will develop the coordination they will need later on as serious athletes.

As pick-up games are created every day in every part of the world, it is impossible to be all-inclusive. Therefore, I hope that this book will grow. I want it to be a book sports enthusiasts can use to find new ways to play their favorite games and where they can share their own creativity with others. If you have invented a pick-up game or if you know of one that hasn't been listed here, please write to me in care of the publisher:

Facts On File, Inc.
c/o D.W. Crisfield
460 Park Avenue South
New York, NY 10016

Note: In the absence of a gender-neutral pronoun, I have used "he" and "his" throughout instead of "he or she." Keep in mind that these words encompass both sexes.

1

BADMINTON

The Game

In badminton it's the bird that makes the game so fun, unique, and challenging. Also known as a shuttlecock in more formal situations, the bird is a cork pierced with feathers or—as in modern backyard sets—a nylon, plastic and rubber model. The rest of the equipment consists of a net and some thin, fragile rackets.

THE DUKE OF BEAUFORT PLAYS BADMINTON

Long before anybody in the Western world had heard of badminton, the remarkably similar game of poona was being played in India. Because India was under British control, it wasn't long before British officers were introduced to the game.

In 1873 the Duke of Beaufort, whose estate was called Badminton, had a party that included several British officers. When bad weather confined all of the guests indoors, one of the officers at the party stuck feathers in a champagne cork and batted it across the dining-room table with a tennis racket to illustrate the game. The bored guests—and even the duke himself—loved the game and grabbed their rackets.

After that, the duke continued to have parties that featured the game as the chief entertainment. People began referring to it as the badminton game, hence the sport was born.

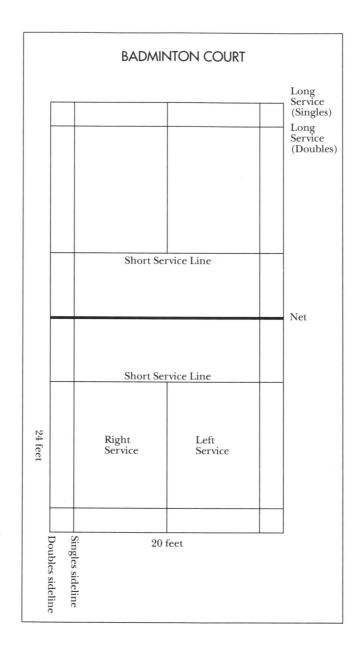

The object of badminton is to volley the shuttlecock back and forth over the net in an effort to reach 15 points. A player wins a point if he is able to place the shuttlecock out of his opponent's reach—yet still in bounds—or if the opponent hits the shuttlecock out of bounds.

The server is the only one who can score. During the serve, the head of the racket must be below the server's hand. Serves start on the right-hand side of the court but then alternate right and left as the serve continues. Court size varies with singles and doubles.

RELAYMINTON

Number of Players: 4
Equipment: racket for each player, shuttlecock, net
Playing Area: backyard
Ages: 8 and up

This is a doubles game for badminton players who really want a lot of exercise. In normal badminton doubles, players take an area of the court and defend it. Partners support one another if one is caught out of position. In Relayminton, players must alternate hits. No matter where the shuttlecock is hit on the court, the player who received it the last time must let his partner hit it. Scoring is the same as in regular badminton.

Dodging a partner and racing to a spot across the court makes this a very strenuous game. For an additional challenge, or if the badminton set has only two rackets, the game can be played with only one racket for each side. A player must hand the racket off to his partner as soon as he hits.

SHUTTLE

Number of Players: 6 or more
Equipment: racket for each player, shuttlecock, net
Playing Area: backyard
Ages: 8 and up

Shuttle is a good game for larger groups. Players divide into two equal teams—one team on each side of the net—and then line up one behind the other.

The first player from one line serves to the other team to start play and then runs to the end of his line. The first player in line on the opponent's team returns the shuttlecock and runs to the end of his line.

The new front person is now the one who fields the serve return, and he also rushes to the end of the line. In other words, a player gets one shot and then lets his teammates play out the rest of the point until he moves to the front of the line again.

The game is played to 10 points. As in RELAYMINTON, limiting each team to one racket can increase the difficulty; teammates must pass the racket to each other before returning the shot.

SOLO SHUTTLE

Number of Players: 6 or more
Equipment: racket for each player, shuttlecock, net
Playing Area: backyard
Ages: 8 and up

The setup of Solo Shuttle is identical to SHUTTLE, with two teams lined up on opposite sides of the net. This time, each player must have his own racket, and

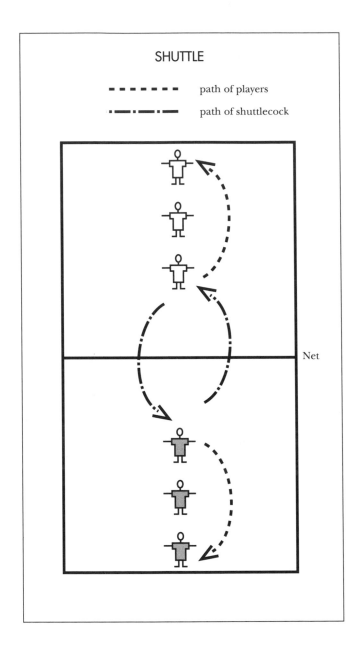

it's not necessary that the teams be exactly equal because they'll constantly be changing anyway.

Play begins as before, with one player serving to the other side. This time, however, the server goes to the end of the line on the opposite side of the court.

There is no score in this game. When a player misses a shot, he is eliminated. The winner is the player who stays on the court after all others have been eliminated. When the game is down to two players, they stay on their own side of the court.

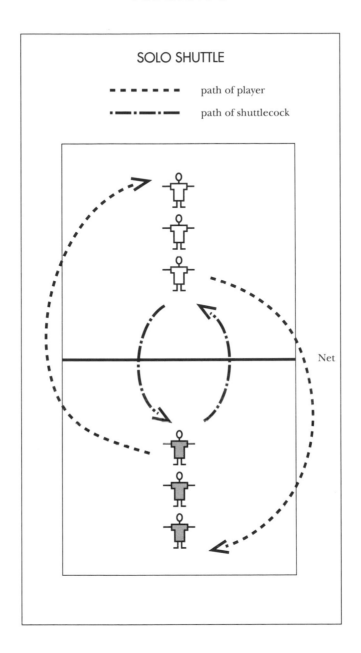

SOLO SHUTTLE

- - - - - - path of player

-·-·-·- path of shuttlecock

Net

TOP OF THE HILL

Number of Players: 4 or more
Equipment: two rackets, one shuttlecock and one net for every two players
Playing Area: backyard
Ages: 10 and up

The number of players determines the number of nets used. For instance, if six players are involved, then there will be three nets. Each side of each net is ranked.

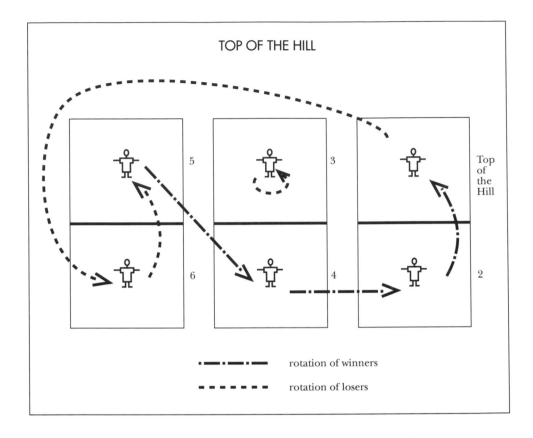

TOP OF THE HILL

Top of the Hill

rotation of winners

rotation of losers

The highest-ranked net—sides 1 and 2—is the "top of the hill." Players draw lots to see who starts on which badminton court.

The higher rank serves to the lower rank. One point is played out. For all places except the top of the hill, the winner of the rally moves to the next court. The loser stays where he is.

At the top of the hill, things are a little different. This is the only place that players can score points, and even then only the winner gets the point. He remains where he is. The loser of this rally goes all the way back to the lowest-ranked spot.

The loser on a court always serves for the next rally. The first player to get 10 points—or the player who has collected the most points at the end of a designated time—is the winner.

TOP OF THE HILL—DOUBLES

Number of Players: 8 or more
Equipment: four rackets, one shuttlecock, and one net for every four players
Playing Area: backyard
Ages: 10 and up

When TOP OF THE HILL is played with doubles teams, it changes slightly. Instead of winning one point, the players must win an entire game, unless the game at

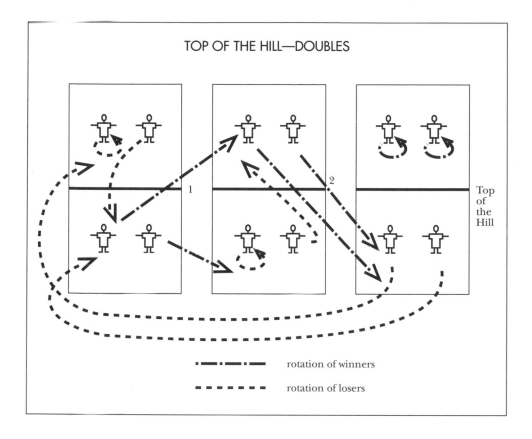

TOP OF THE HILL—DOUBLES

Top of the Hill

·—·—·—·   rotation of winners

·· ·· ·· ··   rotation of losers

the top of the hill is over first. If it is, all other games end and the winning team is the one with the most points. If a game is tied, one more point may be played.

Rotation is slightly different too. As before, the top-of-the-hill winners stay where they are and the top-of-the-hill losers go to the last-ranked net, but this time they split up the team, one on each side of the net. The winners and losers of the other games also split up, unless they are about to enter the top-of-the-hill court—in which case they stay together. Otherwise rotation remains the same.

P O P C O R N

Number of Players: 3 or more
Equipment: racket for each player, shuttlecock
Playing Area: anywhere
Ages: 6 and up

Popcorn can be played anywhere, but it's best if there are definite boundaries. Players stand inside this marked-off area. Each player counts off, so each has a different number. Player 1 starts with the shuttlecock and hits it up in the air. Player 2 must then hit it up in the air again for player 3, and so on.

The shuttlecock must always go up first—no smashes to the ground are allowed—but a player may hit it in any direction. If the player misses the shuttlecock, then he is eliminated. Boundaries help because then a player can't hit a completely unreachable shot. The last player left is the winner.

BALLOONMINTON

Number of Players: 2 or 4
Equipment: racket for each player, net, balloons
Playing Area: backyard
Ages: 6 and up

Balloonminton is a less serious form of badminton. It doesn't work if the day is too windy or if the supply of balloons is fairly limited. The game is played exactly the same way as regular badminton except that a balloon is used as a replacement for the shuttlecock.

Different sizes of balloons, different amounts of air in them, and the addition of water will all affect how the balloons move. Players can experiment and see which kind of Balloonminton is most fun for them.

KEEP IT UP

Number of Players: 1 or more
Equipment: racket, shuttlecock
Playing Area: anywhere
Ages: 6 and up

This game can be played alone or with other players. The object is to hit the shuttlecock in the air as many times as possible without letting it hit the ground. This won't be very challenging for more experienced players, but it is an excellent game for building eye-hand coordination among beginners.

If only one person is playing, then he should set a goal and try to beat his highest number each time. If more than one person is playing simultaneously, then the winner is the player who can keep the shuttlecock up the longest.

SOLO VOLLEY

Number of Players: 1
Equipment: racket, shuttlecock, net
Playing Area: backyard
Ages: 10 and up

Sometimes a player is stuck all by himself and just dying to play a game. This is the time for Solo Volley. The player starts on one side of the net and hits a high lob to the other side; he then dashes under the net to retrieve his own shot. If he's successful, he hits it back to the first side, then again darts under the net. As long as the player keeps the hits high, not deep, he will get quite a workout and have a fun game as well.

2

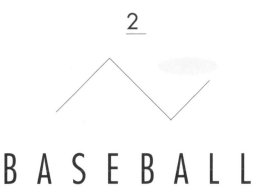

BASEBALL

The Game

Legend has it that Abner Doubleday invented the game of baseball in Cooperstown, New York, but solid evidence reveals that this most definitely was not the case.

   Actually, baseball might have been invented as early as 3000 B.C.; the Egyptians, Greeks and Romans were all known to have played games that used a bat. Most likely, however, the game as we know it evolved from two British games, cricket and rounders.

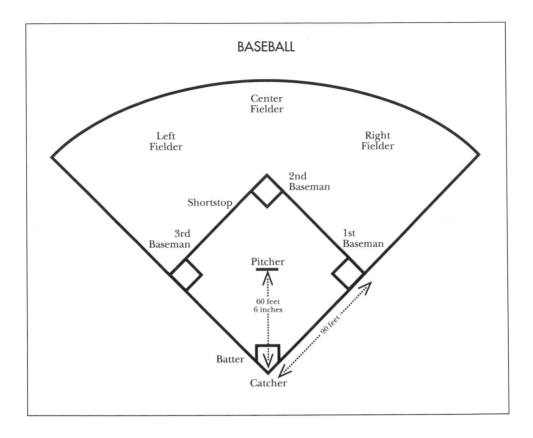

BASEBALL

Center
Fielder

Left
Fielder

Right
Fielder

2nd
Baseman

Shortstop

3rd
Baseman

1st
Baseman

Pitcher

60 feet
6 inches

90 feet

Batter

Catcher

The one fact we can be sure of is that the official rules of baseball were set down in the 1840s by a man named Alexander Cartwright. There were actually quite a few rules to set down; baseball is one of the more elaborate sports. The field consists of the infield—which is made up of three bases and home plate, one at each corner of a diamond—and the outfield, which usually extends beyond the infield to the homerun wall or fence.

There are nine players on each team, and when one team is up to bat, the other team is out in the field playing defense in the following positions: pitcher, catcher, first baseman, second baseman, shortstop, third baseman, left fielder, center fielder and right fielder. In Little League there is a tenth position, short center field, located behind second base.

The object of the game is for the batting team to hit the ball safely, make it around all of the bases and cross home plate (or "score") without being put out. A run may be achieved in one swing (a "homerun") or through several players driving in their teammates who have reached a base. Batters can reach a base by walking (receiving four bad pitches), hitting a single, double or triple, or by getting hit by a wild pitch.

Outs can happen in a number of ways: A batter may strike out (swing and miss or get called out on three good pitches); a fielder may catch the batted ball in the air; a fielder may pick the ball up and tag the runner before the runner reaches the base; a fielder, holding the batted ball, may tag the base before the batter does; and a fielder may throw the ball to the base before the batter reaches it. After three outs, the teams switch sides.

After each team has been up to bat, one inning has been completed. The entire game consists of nine innings, unless there is a tie, in which case the game goes into "extra innings" until the tie is broken.

SCRUB BALL

Number of Players: 6 or more
Equipment: baseball glove for each player
Playing Area: field with one base and home plate
Ages: 10 and up

Scrub Ball is a minigame of baseball that is great to play when there are only a few players. The infield consists of just one base and home plate; there are no teams in Scrub Ball, just positions. The positions go in order: batter 1, batter 2, catcher, pitcher, baseman, fielder. If there are more players then they go into more fielding positions—fielder 2, fielder 3, and so on.

Each player plays for himself, but batter 1 and batter 2 often must work together to get each other from first base to home. Outs are made in the same manner as baseball. If a batter gets out, all players move forward in position and the batter who is out becomes the fielder. The other batter stays where he is and plays with a new teammate.

Players keep track of the number of runs they score individually. At the end of a designated time, the player with the most runs is the winner. This game also can be played without keeping score, just allowing everyone a chance to play different positions and get up to bat.

THREE TEAM BALL

Number of Players: 6
Equipment: bat, baseball, glove for each player
Playing Area: field with one base and home plate
Ages: 10 and up

Three Team Ball is a variation on SCRUB BALL that allows the players to have a teammate, so they don't have to play solo.

In this case, batter 1 and batter 2 are a team, pitcher and catcher are a team and the baseman and fielder are a team. The team at bat is given two outs. The other two teams have to work together to get them out. When this happens the players rotate positions as a unit: the batters become the fielder and first baseman; the fielder and first baseman become the pitcher and catcher; and the pitcher and catcher become the batters.

The game is played for nine two-out innings, but now the innings have a top, middle and bottom.

HOME RUN DERBY

Number of Players: 2 or more
Equipment: bat, baseball, glove for each player
Playing Area: field with designated home run area
Ages: 8 and up

With two player Home Run Derby, one player pitches and the other bats. Each time the batter hits the ball into the designated home run area (often a fence is used), the batter gets one point. Any other hit is counted as an out. As in regular baseball, half of the inning is over after three outs. The pitcher and batter switch positions. The player with the most points after nine innings is the winner.

If there are three players, they all play against each other, with the third player retrieving the hit balls. Each player rotates into each position, but now, as in THREE TEAM BALL, instead of just a bottom and top half of an inning, innings have a bottom, top and middle.

With four or more players, it's best to divide into two teams. The teams still switch sides after every half inning, the pitcher and the retriever alternate every inning, and the two batters alternate every at bat.

STOOLBALL

Number of Players: 2 or more (better with more)
Equipment: bat, rubber ball, four stools
Playing Area: backyard
Ages: 8 and up

Stoolball was invented over 600 years ago in Europe, but it still can be a great game played today. An upturned stool is placed behind the batter (where the catcher would be). The pitcher must hit the stool with the soft rubber ball that is used. The batter must hit the ball with the bat before the ball hits the stool. Then, in order to score a run, the batter must run to the three other stools that are placed around the field (like bases) and home again. He may not stop at any of the stools. If the other players hit the runner—or hit the stool in front of the runner—with the ball, the runner is out and the next, or other, person is up to bat.

TRIANGLE BALL

Number of Players: 4 or more
Equipment: bat, baseball, glove for each player
Playing Area: triangle-shaped field with two bases
Ages: 8 and up

The boundaries, which form the shape of a triangle, must be clearly marked for this game, so it's a good idea to play it in the dirt, where lines can be dug, or on the pavement, where lines can be drawn. Home plate and the two bases are at each corner of the triangle.

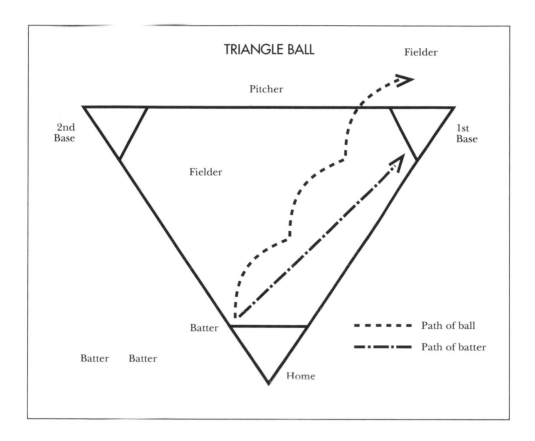

TRIANGLE BALL

Players divide into two equal teams, one up to bat and one out in the field. One of the fielding players pitches the ball from the top edge of the triangle toward the batter. In order for the batter to get a hit, the hit ball must bounce at least once within the triangle. If it doesn't, then the batter is out.

If, however, the batter gets a ball to bounce within the triangle, then he takes off for first base, and possibly second or home, if it was an exceptionally good hit. The fielders try to field the ball and tag either the base or the runner, just as in regular baseball. Three outs and the teams switch sides. The team with the most runs after nine innings is the winner.

HORSE

Number of Players: 2 or more
Equipment: bat, bucket of baseballs
Playing Area: field
Ages: 10 and up

Although there are not many baseball games that need as few as two people. Horse is one of them, and it's a great game for honing placement skills.

The first player decides on the type of hit he is going to make, such as a grounder, line drive, fly ball, bunt, and so on, and where he is going to hit it, such as down the third base line, into center field, between first and second, wherever. He then tosses a ball into the air and attempts that particular hit.

If he makes the hit he described, then the next player must duplicate it exactly. If the second player is able to accomplish this, then the first player (or the third player if there are more than two) must duplicate it again. This goes on until someone misses. That person gets an "H" and the next person in line makes up the next shot. Play continues in this manner until someone has spelled out H-O-R-S-E. That player is the loser, and the other player(s) wins.

PINBALL

Number of Players: 3 to 7
Equipment: bat, baseball, four bowling pins, glove for each player
Playing Area: backyard
Ages: 8 and up

Four bases are set up for this game. The more players, the less space is needed between each base. For instance, a game with eight players would have the bases closer together than a game with only four playing.

On each base is a bowling pin. Obviously, most people don't have bowling pins laying around the house, so a similarly weighted item, such as a tennis ball can, can be used instead.

Each player is out for himself. One person is batter, one is pitcher and the rest are fielders. The pitcher throws the ball and the batter hits it. The batter must sprint all of the way around the bases on the outside of the pins and back home again before the fielders knock over each pin by rolling or throwing the baseball into it. The pins must be knocked over in order (first base, second base, third base, home).

There are no balls or strikes. The batter stands at the plate until he hits the ball. However, if the batter lets too many balls go by, there is a good chance that one will knock the home plate pin over. This is an automatic out. The fielding team can get a batter out in three different ways. The pitcher can knock the home plate pin over, as was just indicated, the fielders can catch a batted fly ball before it hits the ground or the fielders can knock all four pins over in order before the batter gets around the bases. The batter also can get himself out if he knocks over one of the pins as he is running or if he fails to run on the outside of the pins.

After three outs, the batter goes to the field, the pitcher becomes the batter and the fielder who is next in line becomes the pitcher.

The player with the most runs at the end of the game is the winner. Games can consist of everyone getting two rounds at bat, three rounds at bat, or 20 rounds at bat. This is completely up to the players.

TEAM PINBALL

Number of Players: 8 or more
Equipment: bat, baseball, four bowling pins, gloves for half the players

BASEBALL

Playing Area: backyard
Ages: 8 and up

This game is almost identical to the last one, and should be played only if there are many players. It's hard to play regular PINBALL if there are 10 people out in the field because it is too easy for the fielders to get to the ball. If this is the case, the players should be divided into two teams. One team is up to bat and the other is out in the field. Play goes for nine innings, as in regular baseball.

DOUBLES

Number of Players: 2 to 4
Equipment: bat, baseball, glove for each player
Playing Area: area with four bases
Ages: 8 and up

Doubles is a great game for a long, narrow backyard. If two or three people are playing, then the game is played with two or three teams of one; if there are four players, then it is played with two teams of two.

After each hit, the batter must get to second base. In other words, he can either hit a double or a homerun. If he gets a double, he stays on second base and hopes his teammate can hit him home. If the batter is the only one on his team, then he leaves a ghost runner on second and goes back to bat. If his next hit is a good one and he gets safely to second, then his ghost runner gets home safely for a run. If the ball is caught in the air or if the ball beats the runner to the base, the runner is out. After three outs, teams switch sides. The team with the most runs at the end of nine innings is the winner.

STOOPBALL

Number of Players: 4 or more
Equipment: baseball or any other type of ball that bounces
Playing Area: steps and a street
Ages: 8 and up

Stoopball evolved in the city, where there wasn't a lot of room to play baseball and where there often wasn't much money to buy equipment. It still works best in a city environment, where the front steps are close to the street, but these days, city streets are often too busy for a game like this. If players can find the perfect Stoopball playing area, though, the game can be a lot of fun.

Players divide into two equal teams, and then everyone but one player from the batting team goes out into the street to field the ball. The batting player stands at the curb. He throws the ball against the stoop so that it bounces out into the street. If it does not make it to the street, it is an out. If the ball is fielded by the opposing team, whether in the air or on the ground, it is also an out. The batting player rotates, and after three outs, the opposing team is up to bat.

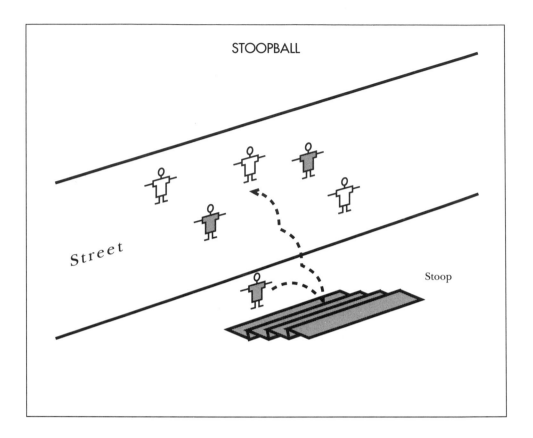

STOOPBALL

Street

Stoop

If, however, the batting team is the team that fields the ball, they get one base for every bounce that the ball takes before being fielded (one bounce is a single, two bounces, a double, three bounces a triple and four a home run). The batting team often has to choose between fielding the ball after a mere single or letting it bounce more for more bases, thereby giving the opposing team greater opportunity to field it themselves for an out.

STEPBALL

Number of Players: 2 or 4
Equipment: baseball or other type of ball
Playing Area: steps and a base
Ages: 8 and up

This is a variation on STOOPBALL, but it needs a little more room because it involves running to a base. On the good side, though, it doesn't need to be played in the street.

If two are playing, then one is the batter and one is the fielder. The batter throws the ball off the steps as hard as he can, hoping the rebound will get past the fielder.

As soon as he throws the ball, the batter takes off toward the base. He must get to the base and back to the steps before the fielder gets the ball and tags him.

If there are two players on each team, then the batter only has to get to the base. It is then up to his teammate to get him back to the steps. Even though it sounds easier not to have to get back to the steps on one turn, it is actually harder because there is another fielder who can get in tagging position while his teammate retrieves the ball.

STOOP

Number of Players: 1
Equipment: baseball or other type of ball
Playing Area: steps
Ages: 8 and up

Stoop is a game for people who are looking to play the two previous games but can't find anyone to play with. A player can entertain himself by playing Stoop and someone is bound to join him.

The opponent in Stoop is the stoop. A player throws the ball off the steps. If it hits the edge of a step and is caught on the fly, the player gets 10 points. If it hits the rising part of the step, bounces down and is then caught on the fly, the player gets one point. If the ball hits the flat part of the step first or is not caught on the fly, the stoop gets a point. The first to reach 100 points is the winner.

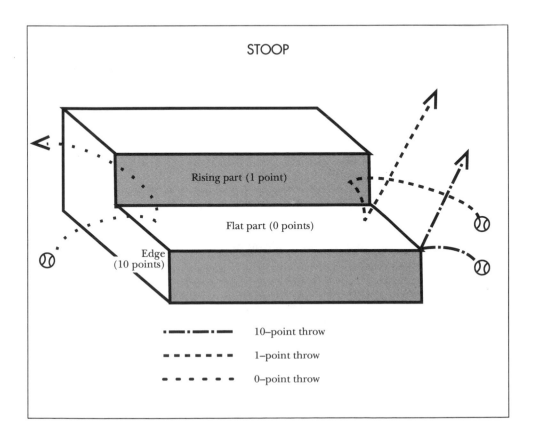

STOOP

Rising part (1 point)

Flat part (0 points)

Edge (10 points)

- · — · — · — · — 10–point throw
- - - - - - 1–point throw
- - - - - - 0–point throw

STOOP FOR TWO

Number of Players: 2
Equipment: baseball or any other type of ball
Playing Area: steps
Ages: 8 and up

In this game, the stoop is no longer a contestant. Players take turns bouncing the ball off the steps, but this time the ball must take one bounce and anyone can catch anyone's throw. The player who makes the catch gets the points.

The points are the same as in the previous game—10 points for a ball that hits the edge and one point for a ball that hits the rising part of the step. If a ball doesn't hit either of those areas, then nobody gets a point.

TARGET

Number of Players: 2 or more
Equipment: baseball, target
Playing Area: anywhere
Ages: 6 and up

The players set up either one target or several targets, which can be a strike zone or bull's-eye area on a wall, a pitchback contraption, a tire swing or simply a mark on the ground that is far away.

Each player gets a turn to pitch or throw the ball. For each throw that hits the target area exactly, a player gets three points. For each throw that gets within a certain range (which can be adjusted depending on the skill of the thrower), a player gets one point. The first player with 15 points wins.

An example would be the tire swing. If a player is able to get the pitch through the tire swing, then he gets three points. If he is able to hit the tire, then he gets one point. It's easier if one player stands on one side of the tire swing and the other stands opposite. That way the players won't spend most of the game retrieving balls. If the players are playing with a pitchback or on a wall, then this obviously isn't an issue.

If the players' only option is a mark on the ground, then they should put two marks far enough apart that they are difficult to reach. One player takes up a position behind each mark and they throw at each other's mark. Three points should be given for lofted throws and one point given for line drives.

TARGET FOR ONE

Number of Players: 1
Equipment: baseball, target
Playing Area: wall or pitchback contraption
Ages: 6 and up

This is the same game as TARGET, but it's a variation that can be used if a player is all by himself. Because there is no one to retrieve the ball, this game works much better with a wall or pitchback than it does with a tire or mark on the ground.

Every time the player hits the target exactly, he gets two points. If he's close to the target (a player might draw a large circle to indicate the boundaries), then it is worth one point. But if the player misses both areas, then the target gets one point. The first to get 100 points wins.

FENCEBALL

Number of Players: 2 or more
Equipment: bat, baseball, gloves for half the players
Playing Area: backyard with fence
Ages: 8 and up

This is an especially good game if the yard or playing area is small. Hitting the ball over the fence is too easy, so it would hardly be worth considering that a homerun. Instead it is called an out.

In Fenceball, players get an opportunity to work on their finesse game instead of their power game. The object is to hit the fence on the fly for a double or on the ground for a single. Everything else is an out, so the fielding team does its best to stop the ball before it reaches the fence.

Players do not run but they keep track of where the batters are and how many runs have scored. After three outs, players switch sides. The game is over after nine innings of play (unless the game is tied).

CALL IT FIRST

Number of Players: 5 or more
Equipment: bat, baseball, glove for each player
Playing Area: field
Ages: 10 and up

One player is up to bat, another is the pitcher and the rest are spread throughout the outfield. The pitcher tosses the ball to the batter. It should not be a hard pitch, because the object is not to strike the batter out. In fact, the batter stays there until he gets a hit, so it's in everyone's best interest to throw an easy pitch.

Before the pitch, however, the batter must call out a person's name first. If the batter hits it to that person, in the air or on the ground, then he can stay up to bat and call out the name of another person. If he misses, then he goes to the right field position, everyone shifts over, and the pitcher goes up to bat.

PICKLE

Number of Players: 3
Equipment: baseball, two gloves
Playing Area: two bases
Ages: 6 and up

This game is also known as Rundown or Hotbox, and it simulates what happens in a real game if a player gets caught in a bad baserunning situation.

Two of the players stand at each base, and the third player is in the middle. The goal of the third player is to get to one of the bases without being tagged with the ball. The players on the bases run at the middle player and toss the ball back and forth to each other in an effort to tag him. If the runner is tagged, then he stays in the middle and tries again. If he makes it to a base, then he takes the place of the person who was on that base. That person now goes in the middle.

5 0 0

Number of Players: 3 or more
Equipment: baseball, bat, glove for each player
Playing Area: field
Ages: 8 and up

500 is a very physical game. One batter hits the ball to the rest of the players in the outfield. The fielders must battle each other for the ball and points. The one who catches a fly ball receives 50 points. A fielded grounder is worth 25 points. The first fielder to reach 500 points total becomes the next batter.

P E P P E R

Number of Players: 4 or more
Equipment: bat, baseball, glove for each player
Playing Area: anywhere
Ages: 10 and up

Pepper is one of the most popular warm-up games for nearly every baseball team, including those in the Major Leagues. It warms the muscles, keeps the reflexes moving and keeps the mind thinking.

One player is the batter. The other three line up in front of him about five feet away. One of these players tosses the ball to the batter who hits it back lightly, either in the air or on the ground.

If a player fields it cleanly, he immediately tosses it back for another hit. This continues until either the batter misses a toss or a fielder misses a hit. If the batter misses, then he goes to the end of the fielding line and the first fielder in line becomes the batter. If a fielder misses, then he goes to the end of the fielding line, and the batter remains the same.

Another variation is to allow the fielders to toss the ball to each other, in addition to tossing it right back to the batter. This might be good strategy if a player toward the head of the line isn't paying attention. If he misses the toss from the other fielder, then he has to go to the end of the line and everyone moves up one. It also tests the batter's reflexes because he doesn't know whether the ball is coming to him or going to another player.

O N E   A   C A T

Number of Players: 3 or more
Equipment: bat, baseball, glove for each player

THE DERIVATION OF THE NAME ONE A CAT

The name of this game came from England. When English players didn't have enough players for rounders or cricket, they created a pick-up game with fewer bases. The bases were called "old cats." With only a few people playing, the game only had one base. It was called "One Old Cat." If more people were playing, there were more bases. The games were then called "Two Old Cat," "Three Old Cat," and so on.

Playing Area: anywhere
Ages: 10 and up

The goal of every player in One a Cat is to remain in the batting position as long as possible, and—if only three or four are playing—there is only one of these coveted batting positions. The other players are the pitcher and fielders.

The batter hits the ball and tries to get to the base (when only a few people are playing, there is only one base) and back home again without getting out. If the fielders or the pitcher is able to throw or tag the batter out, then the players all rotate: The pitcher becomes the batter; the fielder becomes the pitcher; and the batter becomes the fielder (or, if there are two fielders, then the batter becomes the second fielder and the second fielder becomes the first fielder). If the batter hits a fly ball, the player who catches it is automatically the batter, and the rest of the players rotate accordingly.

With five or six people, it's best to use two bases and two batters. Now that there is another batter behind him, a player has two chances to get home. It's just as difficult though, because even if the player gets safely to first base on his hit and safely to second base on the next batter's hit, he is still out because he did not get home in the two chances.

With more players, three batters can be up and the entire baseball field can be used. With three batters and the whole field, a player has three chances to get home.

THREE FLIES UP

Number of Players: any number
Equipment: bat, baseball, glove for each player
Playing Area: field
Ages: 8 and up

This is a very simple game, but kids seem to play it for hours. The appeal is probably because it is among the most physical variations of baseball.

One player is the batter. Everyone else takes a position in the outfield. The batter hits fly balls and the outfielders try to catch them. The first outfielder who catches three flies is up to bat. Needless to say, there is a fair amount of pushing and elbowing in order to be the one who catches the ball. No score is kept, so it can go on for hours.

DERBY BALL

Number of Players: 4
Equipment: bat, baseball, glove for each player
Playing Area: half of a baseball field
Ages: 10 and up

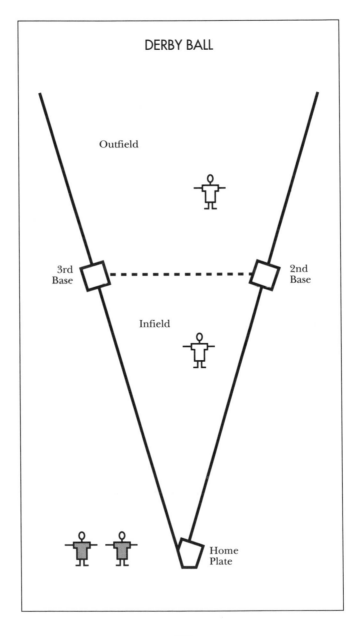

BASEBALL

This game is one of the best variations of baseball. It is played on only half of the field, between second and third base.

One team is up to bat and the other is out in the field. One fielder is an infielder and the other is an outfielder. The batter throws the ball up to hit it (or the infielder can play pitcher). There is no baserunning. If the ball gets past the infielder on the ground, it is a single. If it goes over his head, it is a double. Past the outfielder on the ground is a triple, and over his head is a homerun. A caught fly ball is an out, as is a ground ball stopped by the infielder.

The batters alternate who comes up to bat, and after three outs the teams switch sides. They play nine innings as in regular baseball.

BOXBALL

Number of Players: 2
Equipment: baseball or any other ball
Playing Area: squares marked in chalk on pavement
Ages: 10 and up

Players should mark off a strip of three boxes. (Three squares on a sidewalk can work.) One player owns one end box, the other player owns the other end box, and the middle box is a strike zone. Players must stand outside their boxes.

The first player comes up to bat. He must toss or throw the baseball so that it bounces into his opponent's box. If it hits the strike zone or misses the box entirely, it is considered a strike. Three strikes equals one out.

If the ball does go into the opponent's box, then the opponent must catch it on one bounce, remembering not to step into the box itself. If the receiving

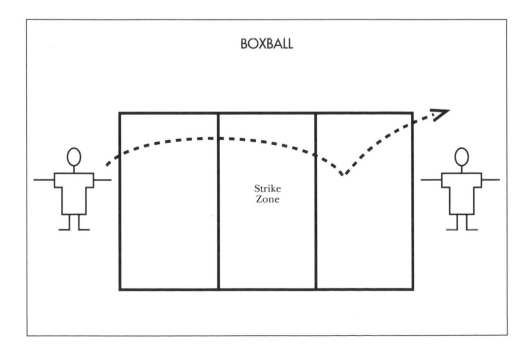

BOXBALL

Strike
Zone

player catches the ball after one bounce, it is considered an out for the throwing player. If he does not catch it after one bounce, then each additional bounce is considered a base for the throwing player—two bounces is a single, three is a double, four is a triple and five is a homerun.

After three outs, it is the other player's turn to throw. The winner is the player with the most runs at the end of nine innings.

If the players become too good at throwing the ball to the opponent—and the scores become awfully high—then the game can be changed to make it more difficult to get a hit. Instead of the batter throwing or tossing the ball, the fielder tosses the ball on one bounce to the batter. The batter must then hit it with his hand into the opponent's box.

ROLLBALL

Number of Players: 2 or more
Equipment: bat, baseball, gloves for half the players
Playing Area: field with one base
Ages: 8 and up

One team goes up to bat, while the other plays the field. There is only one base, but the batter must run to the base and back again in one turn. If he is successful, he gets a run.

After the batter hits the ball, the fielders retrieve it and try to get him out. The only way to get an out is by rolling the ball toward the dropped bat and hitting it before the batter makes it to the base and back. After three outs, the teams switch sides. The team with the most runs after nine innings is the winner.

BUNK BASEBALL

Number of Players: 2 or more
Equipment: rubber ball or tennis ball
Playing Area: indoor area with rafter or similar ledge
Ages: 8 and up

Bunk Baseball is the perfect rainy day or evening activity at camp, but it can be played anytime. Players divide into two equal teams. The idea is to get the ball to bounce on a rafter. One bounce is a single, two bounces a double and so on.

But getting the ball to bounce isn't the only requirement. Even if the ball bounces four times, it's not a homerun unless the person who threw it up there catches it as it comes off the rafter.

Players must be sure to keep track of where the "runners" are on base. For instance, if a player gets a two-bouncer (a double) and then a one-bouncer (a single), he will have one player on third and one player on first.

If the person fails to catch the ball or if the ball misses the beam entirely, it's an out. Three outs and it is the other team's turn to toss. As in regular baseball, play goes on for nine innings, and the team with the most runs is the winner.

BASEBALL

BUNTBALL

Number of Players: 8 to 10
Equipment: bat, baseball, gloves for half the players
Playing Area: infield
Ages: 12 and up

Buntball is a minigame of baseball, which allows players to work on their bunting skills. An outfield is not really needed for this game; while a first baseman, second baseman, third baseman, pitcher and catcher are ideal, the game can be played without the second baseman.

The batter's only option is to bunt, either down the first- or third-base line. Fielders must start behind the base; if they leave their area before the batter hits the ball, then the batter gets a free base.

Other than that, the game is the same as baseball: Three strikes and the player is out; three outs and the teams switch sides. Nine innings are played, and the team with the most runs at the end is the winner.

LINE-UP

Number of Players: 6 or more
Equipment: bat, baseball, gloves for half the players
Playing Area: field
Ages: 12 and up

This game uses only one base and home plate, but the base is considerably farther away from home plate than a normal base would be. The distance can be approximately one and a half times as much, but it's up to the players.

Players divide into two equal teams, one in the field and one up to bat. The ball is pitched, and the batter takes off for the base as soon as he hits it. If he gets there safely, he may decide to run home again or he may decide to stay.

Then it's the next batter's turn. When this batter hits the ball, he also runs to the base. The player already on the base may decide to run home or may decide to stay. An unlimited number of players may be lined up behind the base waiting for an opportunity to run home. When the opportunity presents itself, one may go, a few may go or all may go. The batting team gets a run for each player who crosses home plate safely.

Once a player leaves the base to head toward home, he must go all of the way. He can't take a lead off the base to see if the ball will be fielded cleanly. Once the runner is headed toward home, the fielders only need to get the ball to home plate to get him out. They do not need to tag him, although this is acceptable.

There are two more points. As in regular baseball, a caught fly ball counts as an out. However, the type of hit is of concern only to the batter. Players on the base may run on any hit, including fly balls that might be caught.

Finally, if all players on the batting side are caught behind the base—with no players left to bat—then the side is automatically out and must go into the field. Obviously, players should take great care to see that this doesn't happen.

SOFTBALL

Number of Players: 18
Equipment: bat, softball, gloves for half the players
Playing Area: softball field
Ages: 8 and up

Softball is a variation of baseball in which the differences, as in WIFFLEBALL, come primarily from the fact that different equipment is used.

The softball is much bigger than the baseball, and the diamond is much smaller. The major difference in the rules is that the ball must be pitched underhanded with the elbow and the wrist the same distance away from the body. (In other words, no sidearm allowed.)

There are two different types of Softball: fast pitch and slow pitch. The fast pitch is more like baseball, because stealing is allowed; but no leads can be taken until the ball has left the pitcher's hand. The slow pitch requires that the ball arc into the air before it crosses the plate. Some slow pitchers can get such a high arc on the fall that it actually comes across the plate almost vertically.

KICKBALL

Number of Players: 8 or more
Equipment: playground ball, soccer ball, or volleyball
Playing Area: baseball field
Ages: 6 and up

Kickball has the exact same rules as baseball, except a larger, softer ball is used, and it is kicked rather than batted. Needless to say, the pitcher rolls the ball instead of throwing it. But there are still strikes and balls. A ball caught in the air is still an out. Nine innings still make up a game. And the team with the most runs at the end of the nine innings is still the winner.

WIFFLEBALL

Number of Players: 2 or more
Equipment: wiffle bat, wiffle ball
Playing Area: anywhere
Ages: 6 and up

It's difficult to describe how Wiffleball is played, because Wiffleball games can be a combination of any of the games mentioned in this chapter. The only difference between those games and Wiffleball is the equipment, which consists of a plastic (and usually hollow) wiffle bat and wiffle ball (usually full of air holes).

Although a full-blown, 18-player game is conceivable, Wiffleball is best played with a small number of players in a backyard or a playground. Probably the most common way of playing is to designate areas for the different types of hits. For example, a single could be a ground ball past the pitcher; a double might be a ball that goes by the pitcher in the air and then hits the ground; a triple could be a ball that hits the side of the house; and a homerun could be any ball that is on the roof. Players adapt the hitting arrangements to suit their playing area.

People remember where the runners are in their heads. There are three types of outs—a strikeout, a ball caught on a fly or a ground ball that didn't make it past the pitcher. Each player or team gets three outs before switching with the other player or team.

PUNCHBALL

Number of Players: 4 or more
Equipment: rubber ball
Playing Area: street
Ages: 8 and up

The essence of Punchball is that it is played in the street, with anything serving as the four bases (a garbage can, a tire, a telephone pole, etc.). The ball used must be rubber (known primarily in Brooklyn by the name "spaldeen"); otherwise, no additional equipment is necessary.

Rather than hit the ball with a long object (as in baseball and WIFFLEBALL), the idea of Punchball is to hit the ball with one hand. There are two variations of the game, one of which should be chosen before the game is started: Batters may either throw the ball up in the air and hit it or bounce it first and then hit it.

Players cover their positions just as in regular baseball, except that there isn't a pitcher. Once the ball is hit in play, the fielding team can get the batter out by catching it on a fly, stepping on a base (or throwing it to a teammate at a base) or tagging him out. Other baseball rules apply, with only slight differences: Each team has three outs an inning; two foul balls (or missed balls) equal an out; the team with the most runs after nine innings wins.

STICKBALL

Number of Players: 2 or more
Equipment: broomstick handle, rubber ball
Playing Area: anywhere, but the street is traditional
Ages: 8 and up

Like WIFFLEBALL, Stickball can be a multitude of games, and what defines it is the equipment—a rubber ball and a broom handle. Traditionally, this was played among the poor kids living in the city who couldn't afford to buy the official equipment. A rubber ball was cheap, and someone could always come up with an old broom handle.

Most often Stickball games just followed standard baseball rules, but variations were created depending on the number of players and the limitations of the playing area. For instance, when there were only a few players (making a full fielding team impossible), the players eliminated baserunning. The goal was to hit the ball by a certain number of manhole covers. One was a single, two a double and so on.

27

ORIGIN OF THE "SPALDEEN"

In Stickball's heyday, it was played on nearly every neighborhood street in New York, and the game had its own language, which was known universally throughout the city. For example, the ball was always called a "spaldeen." This was a variation on the brand name "Spaulding," which made a lot of the balls. Even if a ball was another brand, it was still called a spaldeen if it was used for a stickball game.

If a pitcher is used, one Stickball rule remains the same no matter what variation people play: The pitcher always throws the ball to the batter on one bounce.

SHOELACES

Number of Players: 6 or more
Equipment: bat, baseball, gloves for half the players
Playing Area: field
Ages: 6 and up

Shoelaces is a humorous adaptation of baseball that is best played at picnics or with smaller children, when serious baseball isn't the issue.

The game is identical to baseball in every sense, except that the players must tie their shoelaces together. Running around the bases is considerably slowed, but then again, so is the fielding. The handicap certainly makes it harder to catch a fly ball.

SNOWBALL

Number of Players: 6 or more
Equipment: bat
Playing Area: field
Ages: 6 and up

When snow hits the ground, it's difficult to play baseball, but Snowball is a great substitute. Players divide into equal teams. The team out in the field consists of a pitcher, a catcher and snowball makers. The batting team consists of batters and runners.

One player comes up to bat, while one of his teammates poises to run in a medium-size circle around the pitcher. Meanwhile, the pitcher and the snowball makers have created a stack of about 15 snowballs. When the pitcher yells "go," he starts throwing the snowballs toward the batter and catcher. At the same time, the runner starts around the circle.

The batter tries to swat the snowballs before they reach the catcher, who may not move from his position behind the batter. The runner keeps going, counting

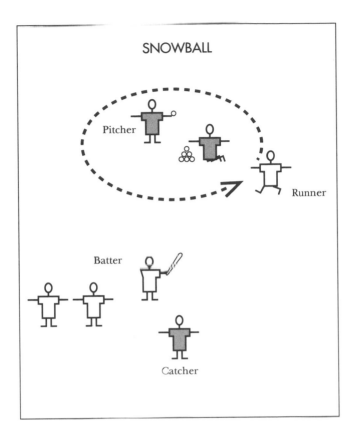

SNOWBALL

his revolutions until the batter misses a snowball. Then the batter is out and the next batter and runner are up. After three outs, the teams change sides.

The pitcher may use only one hand and may throw only one snowball at a time, but he may throw the snowballs as fast as he wants. At the end of nine innings, the team that has completed the most revolutions around the circle is the winner.

3

B A S K E T B A L L

The Game

Basketball is the new kid on the block in the sports realm. Unlike most games, which evolved slowly from games that are centuries old, basketball was deliberately invented in 1891 by a YMCA instructor named James Naismith as an indoor sport that could fill the time between football and baseball.

The object of basketball is to score the most points by throwing the ball through one of the baskets. Today these are nets—not real baskets—but

---

BASKETBALL: A CONSTANTLY CHANGING SPORT

The addition of the three-point shot is a good example of basketball's constantly evolving nature. In fact, there have been so many changes in the game that James Naismith would hardly recognize it.

For instance, in the beginning days of basketball, there was a jumpball after every basket, which slowed the game considerably and gave the taller team a distinct advantage. And because peach baskets were used, people had to be positioned on ladders next to the basket to retrieve the ball so play could continue. Talk about slowing the game down.

Today the National Basketball Association has even added a shot clock, which forces players to get a shot off in a mere 24 seconds. Obviously there can be no stalling; the game of basketball has become one of the fastest sports in existence. ○

---

when the game was invented, peach baskets were used, hence the name "basket-ball."

In the official game, there are two teams of five players each. Play begins with a jump ball. Two players (usually the tallest) face each other in the center of the court, while the referee tosses the ball in the air. The players jump for the ball and try to bat it to a teammate. Once possession is determined, the teams set up their offensive and defensive positions.

To move the ball up the court, players must either pass to a teammate or dribble (bounce the ball on the floor with one hand without pausing to catch it). Players with the ball may not move unless they are dribbling, and once they've stopped, they may not start dribbling again, but instead must pass or shoot. Teams often have intricate offensive plays to create the best opportunity for a shot.

Tactics for defense also vary from team to team, including strategies such as man-to-man, zone, or box and one. Regardless of its methods, the team on defense does anything legal to gain possession: steal a pass, block a shot or get the rebound from a missed shot.

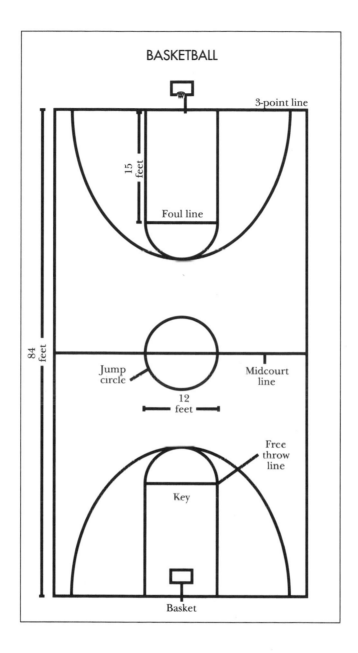

BASKETBALL

3-point line

15 feet

Foul line

84 feet

Jump circle

Midcourt line

12 feet

Free throw line

Key

Basket

If a player holds, pushes, charges or hits another player, he has committed a foul. The fouled player is then given one, two, or three free shots, known as foul shots. These are taken from the foul line (also called the free throw line) and are worth one point.

Baskets made in normal play are worth two points if they are within the arc indicated on the floor and three points if they are outside it. The three-point option was developed fairly recently, and it has given the game an exciting new dimension, with players having to choose between the safe two pointer or the more valuable, yet riskier, three pointer.

HORSE

Number of Players: 2 or more
Equipment: basketball
Playing Area: half court
Ages: 8 and up

Probably the most well known of all pick-up basketball games, Horse can't be beaten for developing excellent and varied shooting skills, even though it doesn't have the fast-paced action of a regular basketball game.

The first player takes a shot from anywhere on the court. If he misses, then the next player may take any shot he pleases. However, if the first player makes the shot, then the next player must duplicate that shot exactly.

If the second player makes this exact same shot, then the first player (or subsequent players) must do the shot again. This goes on until someone misses; that person gets an "H." The next person in line decides which shot will be attempted next. Play continues in this manner until someone has spelled out H-O-R-S-E and is the loser. The other players continue until only one is left.

Shots don't have to be the conventional "jump shot from the corner" or "lay-up from the left-hand side." Players can be as creative as they want and even do a one-handed underhand shot with their back facing the basket.

HOTSHOT

Number of Players: 2
Equipment: basketball, chalk or tape to mark spots, timer
Playing Area: half court
Ages: 8 and up

With chalk or tape, players mark different spots around the court. There should be a few spots near the top of the playing area (three-point distance), a few spots

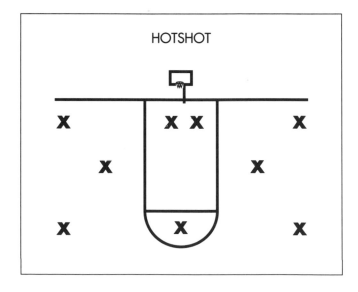

HOTSHOT

on either side of the key (the area between the free-throw line and the basket), one from the free-throw line, a couple of shots from the baseline and a couple of lay-up spots.

One player is the shooter and the other is the timer. A shooter gets points for each basket he makes. A lay-up is worth one point, the baseline and free-throw shots are worth two points, the shots from the side of the key are three points and the shots from far out are worth four points.

The catch is that a player can shoot only two lay-ups at a time, and then he must go on to another shot. Once he takes another shot, he can go back and shoot two more lay-ups. The shooter also must get his own rebound.

The other player clocks the 60 seconds and keeps track of the shooter's points out loud. At the end of the time period, they trade places. The winner is the shooter who has scored the most total points in the allotted time.

BOLF

Number of Players: 2 or more
Equipment: basketball, chalk or tape to mark spots
Playing Area: half court
Ages: 8 and up

Bolf is a combination of basketball and golf, and if you play it after HOTSHOT, you can use the same spots marked on the ground.

In this game, the spots are called "holes." The idea is to make a basket from each of the holes in the fewest shots. The player who successfully completes all of the holes with the fewest shots is the winner.

AROUND THE WORLD

Number of Players: 2 or more
Equipment: basketball, chalk or tape to mark spots
Playing Area: half court
Ages: 8 and up

Like HOTSHOT and BOLF, Around the World uses spots marked on the court; but in this game they are a little more defined. One spot is on each side of the basket in the lay-up position. the other spots form a big arc going around the basket.

The first player starts with a lay-up on one side. If he makes the shot, he goes on to the next point. If he misses, then he can take a chance anywhere on the court. If the chance shot goes in, the player continues on to the next marked spot. If, however, the chance shot misses, the player's turn is over and he must start from the beginning on his next turn. A chance shot can be declined, however, which means the player ends his turn but can remain at the achieved spot on his next turn. The game ends when one person gets all of the way around.

There are even variations of this game. It can be played without the chance shot. It also can be played with two chance shots, with the first miss sending the player back only one spot and the second sending the player all the way back to

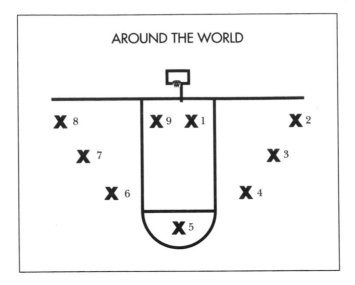

AROUND THE WORLD

the beginning. Players could specify that lay-ups have to be done with the left hand. The more creative, the more fun Around the World can be.

UNIVERSE

Number of Players: 2 or more
Equipment: basketball
Playing Area: half court
Ages: 10 and up

A game that combines aspects of both HORSE and AROUND THE WORLD is Universe. Like Around the World, players take designated shots in order, and if they miss the "chance" shot, they go back to the beginning.

The total number of shots is limited to 12. In order the shots include: the Sun shot, the Mercury shot, the Venus shot, the Earth shot, the Mars shot, the Jupiter shot, the Saturn shot, the Uranus shot, the Neptune shot, the Pluto shot, the Milky Way shot, and the Universe shot. The shots are not picked at the beginning as they are in Around the World but, like Horse, they are made up as play goes on.

For instance, the first player might choose to do a running hook shot in front of the basket. The Sun shot therefore becomes a running hook shot for the rest of the game. If he makes the Sun shot, he can create the Mercury shot—perhaps a jump shot to the left of the foul line. If he makes that he decides on the Venus shot. If he misses it, he can stop and take a "chance." Even if the player misses and has to go back to the beginning, the Sun shot and the Mercury shot have been designated as a running hook shot in front and a jump shot from the left side, respectively. The second player must complete those exact two before he can make up the Venus (or any other) shot. The first player to complete all 12 shots is the winner.

BASKETBALL

HALFCOURT

Number of Players: 2, 4 or 6
Equipment: basketball
Playing Area: half court
Ages: 8 and up

Halfcourt is merely the game of basketball without the full complement of players. If only two players are around, they play against each other in a one-on-one game. If there are four, it's two on two; if there are six, it's three on three.

While the rules of basketball apply to these minigames, a few modifications are usually added to accommodate the smaller area and the smaller number of players. To begin with, players must call their own fouls, so the game is as rough or as polite as the people playing it.

Play goes to 21, and each basket is worth only one point. There are no foul shots or any three pointers. When a basket is made or a player from the defensive team catches a rebound, the team then in possession of the ball must bring it back behind the foul line before driving to the basket or taking a shot (to make it more like a full court game).

MAKE IT, TAKE IT

Number of Players: 2, 4 or 6
Equipment: basketball
Playing Area: half court
Ages: 8 and up

This is a variation of HALFCOURT that evolved in the inner cities where courts were limited and the ability of players varied tremendously.

The difference between Halfcourt and Make It, Take It occurs after the basket. In Halfcourt, the defensive team takes the ball back behind the foul line after a basket is made. In Make It, Take It, the team that makes the basket is the team that gets possession of the ball. In other words, if a team is successful in making its shots and collecting the rebounds of missed shots, it could get to 21 before the other team ever gets to play offense.

In the city, usually the winning team stays on the court and plays any challengers. By playing Make It, Take It, good teams can quickly get rid of challengers who have very little skill. It doesn't seem quite fair for the less-skilled players, but then again, it doesn't waste the good players' time.

TOP OF THE HILL

Number of Players: 8 or more
Equipment: one basketball for every four players
Playing Area: one hoop for every four players
Ages: 10 and up

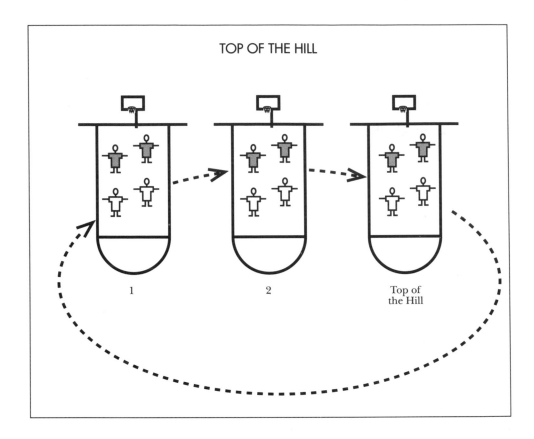

TOP OF THE HILL

1

2

Top of
the Hill

At first glance, Top of the Hill looks to be your basic two-on-two pick-up game. But there's a difference. Top of the Hill is actually many two-on-two pick-up games.

There should be one hoop for every four players. Each hoop is ranked, with the highest rank being called the top of the hill. Players draw lots to see which hoop they start on.

Every time a team wins, its players move up to the next higher ranked court and split up. The losing team stays where it is and the team is split up. In other words, a loser and a winner play together against the other loser and winner.

At the top of the hill, things are a little different. The winners stay where they are and, unlike the winners of the other games, they earn a point for every victory. Even winners who had moved up from the previous net stay together at the top of the hill.

Losers at the top of the hill go to the last-ranked hoop and split up as usual. They play with the split-up losers of the game previously played there.

Each game goes to five, but when the top-of-the-hill game is over, all other games also must end. Players keep track of the points they win at the top of the hill. The player with the most points at the end of the time period is the winner.

BASKETBALL

SQUIRRELS

Number of Players: 6 or more
Equipment: one basketball for every two players, a whistle
Playing Area: full court
Ages: 5 and up

This game is especially good for younger children, because it helps them learn skills, without really noticing it, while playing a game.

Some players spread out all over the court and raise their hands; they are known as trees. One player is the big, bad dog (often the coach), who roams the court. Everyone else is a squirrel. Each squirrel has an acorn (the basketball), which he must dribble constantly.

The squirrels begin the game by touching a tree. They are safe from the big, bad dog when they are in the trees. The big, bad dog has a whistle, though, and whenever he uses it, the squirrels must all change trees while dribbling their acorns. This is when the big, bad dog can tag them. If a squirrel is captured, then he must take the place of a tree, and the tree becomes a squirrel.

In addition, if a squirrel ever stops dribbling while he's in a tree—or if he goes to the same tree instead of changing trees—then he also must change places with the tree.

TWENTY-ONE

Number of Players: 2 or more
Equipment: basketball, chalk
Playing Area: half court
Ages: 8 and up

This game is very easy to learn. A line or an arc is drawn on the pavement, usually around the free throw line. For more advanced players it can be drawn by the three-point arc.

The first player takes a shot from behind the line. If he makes it, he gets three points. If not, he rushes in to get the rebound and takes a second shot from the place where he retrieves the ball, no matter where it is. If he makes this shot, he gets two points. Finally, the player takes the ball in for a lay-up, which counts as one point. In other words, each time the player has a turn, he has the opportunity to get a total of six points.

Then it's the next player's turn. Play continues until a player reaches 21 points. However, players must reach 21 exactly or else they have to start over at zero again. Therefore, if a player has 19 points, he must deliberately miss the shot from behind the line and his lay-up shot.

MUSH BALL

Number of Players: 2 or more
Equipment: basketball

Playing Area: half court
Ages: 8 and up

Sometimes Mush Ball is called Animal Ball because the game can get pretty physical. To start the game, the ball gets thrown against the backboard. All of the players jump for the rebound at once. Whoever gets the rebound puts it back up for a shot. If he misses, everyone goes after the ball again; but if it goes in, then the person who took the shot gets two points and goes to the foul line. The player takes foul shots, getting one point for each one that goes in, until he misses. Then Mush Ball starts all over again with the rebound. The first person to reach 21 points is the winner.

D U C K

Number of Players: 8 or more
Equipment: basketball for each player
Playing Area: court
Ages: 5 and up

Players, each dribbling a ball in front of them, form a large circle. One player is the duck. he dribbles around the outside of the circle and then stops between two players. These two players take off around the circle, dribbling in opposite directions. The duck takes one of the player's positions, and the person who dribbles the fastest around the circle takes the other. The slower person gets a "D" and now becomes the duck. The game is over when a person has spelled D-U-C-K.

F R E E T H R O W S

Number of Players: 2
Equipment: basketball
Playing Area: half court
Ages: 10 and up

The purpose of this game is obviously to build skill in shooting free throws, yet still have fun. One player stands at the free-throw line. The other stands under the basket for the rebound. Every time the free-throw shooter makes a basket, he gets two points and the ball back. If he misses, the other player grabs the rebound and takes a shot from where he recovered the ball. This shot is worth one point if he makes it, and now the players change places.

The first player to reach 21 wins, and like the game TWENTY-ONE, the players must hit 21 exactly or go back to zero.

L A Y I N , S T A Y I N

Number of Players: 2 or more
Equipment: basketball for each player
Playing Area: half court
Ages: 8 and up

This is a very simple elimination game. Players get in a line one behind the other. The first person dribbles in, makes a lay-up and then goes to the end of the line. The rest of the players do the same thing, one at a time.

If a player misses the lay-up, then he is eliminated. The player remaining after all the players have been eliminated is the winner. Variations could include a left-handed lay-up or a reverse lay-up.

SHOOT AND REBOUND

Number of Players: 4 or more
Equipment: at least two basketballs
Playing Area: half court
Ages: 8 and up

Shoot and Rebound is a variation of LAY IN, STAY IN, except that in this game there are two lines and players remain on the court after they are eliminated, so there is less boredom for those who miss early.

Players form two lines; one is the shooting line and one is the rebounding line. The first player from the shooting line dribbles in and takes a lay-up, while the player from the rebounding line comes in to get the rebound. The players then go to the end of the opposite line.

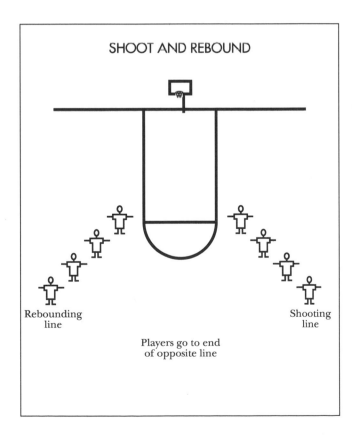

SHOOT AND REBOUND

Rebounding line

Shooting line

Players go to end of opposite line

If a player misses his lay-up, however, he goes to the rebounding line and stays there, rebounding all of time. The last player left in the shooting line is the winner. This game also can be played with jump shots instead of lay-ups.

SUPERMAN

Number of Players: 2
Equipment: basketball, timer
Playing Area: half court
Ages: 8 and up

This is a great game for someone who wants to perfect the quick lay-up. One player is the timer and the other is the shooter. The shooter has 30 seconds to make as many lay-ups as possible.

The hitch, however, is that the shooter must alternate the right and left sides each time he takes a shot. He also must get his own rebounds. If the player is more skilled, then it's good to require that the right-side lay-ups are done with the right hand and the left-side lay-ups are done with the left hand.

At the end of 30 seconds, the timer and the shooter trade duties. The player with the most baskets at the end of a set period wins.

SUPERBOUNDER

Number of Players: 2
Equipment: basketball, timer
Playing Area: backboard or wall
Ages: 8 and up

Superbounder is a variation of SUPERMAN, but this time the player is working on the quick rebound, not the quick lay-up. The nice thing about Superbounder is that a basketball hoop isn't needed for play.

Again, one player is the timer and the other is the rebounder. The rebounder stands on the right side of the net and tosses the ball off the backboard so it will rebound off the left side. As soon as he tosses the ball, the rebounder should leap over to the left side to catch his own rebound. Then he tosses it back over to the right.

The rebounder must do 40 rebounds, while the other player times how long it takes him. Then the other player does 40 rebounds. The player who takes the least amount of time to do it is the winner.

This is an exhausting game. The range of movement is considerably greater than that of the Superman game. If players find themselves too exhausted to do a quality rebound, they should reduce the number of rebounds.

SIXTY-SECOND SHOT

Number of Players: 3
Equipment: basketball, timer
Playing Area: half court
Ages: 10 and up

Sixty-second Shot is almost a combination of SUPERMAN and SUPERBOUNDER, and it's terrific because it emphasizes shooting, rebounding and passing. In this game there is a shooter, a rebounder and a timer. The players rotate their positions after each 60-second round is over.

The shooter stands beyond the free-throw line. The rebounder is positioned under the basket with the ball. The clock starts when the ball is passed to the shooter. The shooter takes a shot and moves to another position on the court. The rebounder grabs the rebound and feeds it out to the shooter again. Play involves catching, shooting, moving to another spot and then switching sides after 60 seconds. The shooter with the most baskets wins.

One of the great things about this game is that the shooter has to move before he can get the ball back, which simulates real basketball play. The problem with many shooting games is that the players generally just stand and shoot, without any gamelike basketball movement.

HOMERUN

Number of Players: 2
Equipment: basketball, chalk
Playing Area: half court
Ages: 10 and up

This is a pick-up game of basketball with a little baseball scoring thrown in. A fairly large arc should be drawn around the basket, beyond the free-throw line. The three-point line can be used if the playing area is a gym.

The first player "up to bat" takes a shot from behind the arc, recovers the ball and takes a shot from the rebound area. If he makes both shots, he gets a homerun. If he misses one of them, it counts as one out. If he misses both, however, it counts as three outs and the other player is up to bat. After nine innings, the player with the most homeruns is the winner.

BULL IN THE RING

Number of Players: 3 or more
Equipment: basketball for each person
Playing Area: anywhere with a hard surface
Ages: 6 and up

Bull in the Ring doesn't need a hoop, so it can be played almost anywhere as long as there are enough basketballs to go around. It's a great game for improving ball-handling skills.

If the playing area is fairly small, as driveways are, then a boundary line does not have to be drawn and the whole playing area can be used. If it's a larger area, say a basketball court, then a small circle or square should be marked off.

The game begins with everyone dribbling simultaneously. The object is to try to tip the other player's basketball outside the playing area. If a player loses his basketball, then he must leave the ring. The last player left in the ring with his basketball is the winner.

This game is good for dribbling skills because players have to be in control, protecting the basketballs with their bodies and looking up at the other players.

BULLS VERSUS COWS

Number of Players: 4 or more
Equipment: one basketball for every two people, timer
Playing Area: small area on court
Ages: 6 and up

If there aren't enough balls to go around for a BULL IN THE RING game, then a modified version called Bulls Versus Cows can be played. Players divide into two teams, the bulls and the cows. Each cow has a ball, while none of the bulls do. The bulls must knock all the cows' basketballs out of the playing area.

A cow who loses his ball is not eliminated. He stays in the ring and is available for a pass from another cow. Players must time how long it takes for the bulls to get rid of all the balls, and then the bulls and cows switch roles. Whoever eliminates the other team's basketballs the fastest is the winner.

TARGET

Number of Players: 2
Equipment: basketball, target (a stick or a coin)
Playing Area: anywhere with a hard surface
Ages: 6 and up

Target helps with accuracy in passing. Players should place some sort of small target between them. A stick or a coin is better than a mark on the surface, because with the latter, it is sometimes hard to tell if the ball actually hit the target.

Players take turns passing the ball in bounce pass fashion back and forth to each other, aiming at the target at the same time. Each time a player hits the target, he gets one point. The game goes to 10, but the victor must win by two.

SPEEDSHOT

Number of Players: 2 or more
Equipment: basketball for each player
Playing Area: half court
Ages: 8 and up

In this game all players shoot at once, which can make things rather confusing. The first shot is from the free-throw line. After that, players just get their rebounds and shoot from there. When a player makes a shot, he yells out the number. The first player to reach seven baskets is the winner.

If you have different-looking basketballs, then each player should have to stay with his own ball. If not, then it's a free-for-all, each person getting the first ball he can.

MONKEY IN THE MIDDLE

Number of Players: 3
Equipment: basketball
Playing Area: anywhere
Ages: 5 and up

The object of this game is for two players to retain possession of the ball for as long as possible, while the third player tries to get it away from them. The two players who have the ball pass it back and forth or dribble without allowing the "Monkey" to steal it.

When the middle player finally does get control, then he switches places with the player who lost the ball in the first place through a bad throw or bad catch. Now that person becomes the monkey in the middle.

CORNERS

Number of Players: 4
Equipment: basketball
Playing Area: square with definite boundaries
Ages: 10 and up

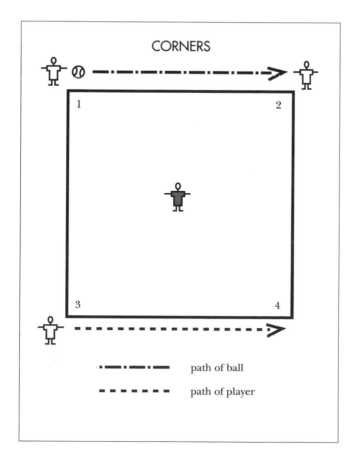

CORNERS

1   2

3   4

·—·—·—· path of ball

- - - - - - path of player

Corners is similar to MONKEY IN THE MIDDLE, except that the outside players are limited as to where their passes can go, and they are not allowed to dribble the ball. This makes it easier for the middle person, although now it is three against one.

The three outside people are positioned on three of the four corners of the square. The middle person stands inside the square. The outside people may pass only along the lines of the square, not across the middle. They also may move only along the lines of the square and not cut across the middle.

To facilitate passing, a player always should have two passing options, which means that the players on the outside of the square are constantly switching corners. For instance, if the ball starts in corner 1, corners 2 and 3 are adjacent and corner 4 is opposite. The other players should be in corners 2 and 3. Then if the ball is passed from corner 1 to corner 2, the player who is in corner 1 stays where he is—adjacent to the corner with the ball—but the player from corner 3 must run over to corner 4 to provide the second passing alternative, because corner 4 is now the adjacent one.

This game is excellent for helping players learn to move into the open position when receiving a pass. If the middle person is able to get the ball away from an outside person, then he and the outside person who made the error switch places.

TRANSITION BALL

Number of Players: 10
Equipment: basketball
Playing Area: full court
Ages: 10 and up

Transition Ball is a good warm-up basketball game for the beginning of the season, when players aren't in good shape. Two players on each team are offense, two are defense and one is the transition player.

The game is played exactly like regular basketball, except that players are confined to a portion of the court. The offense has the offensive half, the defense has the defensive half, and the transition players can move between the two keys

THE WOMEN'S GAME

Girls and women played a game similar to TRANSITION BALL for most of this century. Originally women played the same basketball game as men until a gym teacher at Smith College decided that the full-court game was too "exhausting" for women.

The teacher modified the game so that the women wouldn't have to run as much. There were six players on a team, three on defense and three on offense. The players couldn't cross the half-court line. Believe it or not, women's basketball remained like this until the 1960s.   o

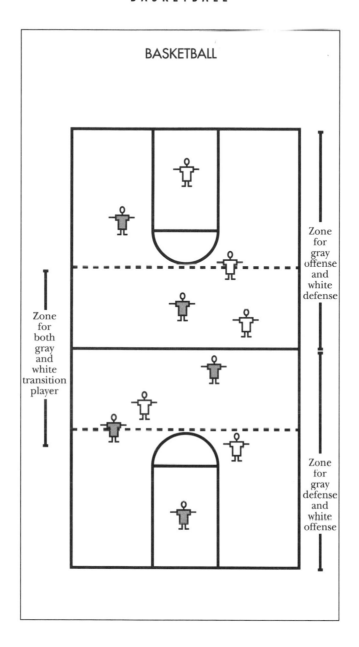

BASKETBALL

Zone for gray offense and white defense

Zone for both gray and white transition player

Zone for gray defense and white offense

(see diagram). In other words, it's a three-on-three game at each end and in the middle of the court. If players move out of their zone, then the other team gets the ball.

GHOSTBALL

Number of Players: 1
Equipment: basketball
Playing Area: half court
Ages: 6 and up

If a player is all by himself and wants a little competition, Ghostball is a great solution. In this game, a ghost is sitting on top of the basket. Every time a player gets the ball by the ghost (into the basket), he gets two points. Every time the ghost gets the ball (the player misses), the ghost gets one point. The first one to reach 21 points is the winner.

The type of shots that the player takes depends on his skill level and what he is trying to accomplish. For instance, a beginning player might play Ghostball with just lay-ups. Someone who wants to work on his outside jump shot might set up marked spots on the court, as in AROUND THE WORLD. For someone having trouble at the foul line, the shots might all be free-throws. A player could even just get the rebound and put the ball back up from wherever it lands.

4

C R O Q U E T

The Game

No one is really sure where croquet started. An early French game called *palle malle* was very similar to what we know as croquet, in that players used wooden mallets to strike wooden balls through metal frames. The game died out, however, before it had a chance to spread around the world. The true origins of croquet as we know it today can only be traced as far back as 1850.

The object of croquet is to hit a wooden ball through the wickets (wire that is bent into a loop and stuck in the ground) that are set up as a course, and be the first to reach the final stake.

In traditional backyard croquet, the first player places the ball at mallet's length from the starting stake. He or she then hits the ball through as many wickets as possible. (Usually the first two can be done together.) A player gets an extra hit for each wicket scored. The next player goes when the previous player runs out of hits.

If a player hits another player's ball, he gets to "send," or "croquet," that player. The player does this by placing his ball next to the opponent's ball and whacking his own ball. If the player does not want his own ball to move (this is usually the case), he may place his foot on his own ball before hitting it. After sending an opponent, a player gets one free stroke. If the player sends the opponent's ball out of bounds, however, then the player must forfeit this free stroke.

Once a player has croqueted an opponent's ball, he is considered "dead" on that ball and may not hit the same one again until he has gone through a wicket. If he does, then his turn ends. A player has to be careful not to become dead on

49

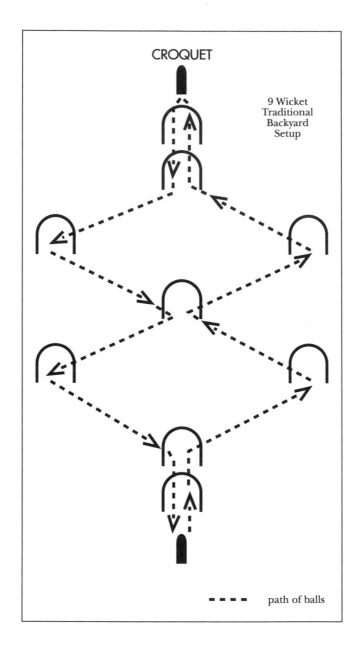

CROQUET

9 Wicket
Traditional
Backyard
Setup

- - - - path of balls

too many balls at once. The opponents will then have extra incentive to keep his ball from going through another wicket.

If a player goes through a wicket and hits a ball at the same time, he must decide if he would like to count the wicket or take the two strokes and become dead on the other ball. He may not do both.

In the traditional backyard croquet arrangement, there are nine wickets and two stakes. This set-up is very adaptable, ranging from a short and fat course to a long and skinny course, depending on the backyard. It can even turn a corner or follow the lines of a peculiar backyard.

INTERNATIONAL CROQUET

Number of Players: 2 to 4
Equipment: a mallet and 4 balls
Playing Area: field with six wickets and one stake
Ages: 6 and up

The nine-wicket, two-stake setup is the most popular in the United States because it is so adaptable; but in croquet competition, International Croquet is the game of choice. It is played with six wickets and one stake.

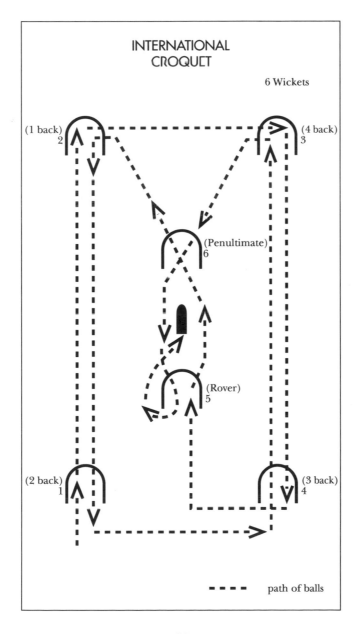

INTERNATIONAL CROQUET

6 Wickets

(1 back) 2

(4 back) 3

(Penultimate) 6

(Rover) 5

(2 back) 1

(3 back) 4

- - - - path of balls

International Croquet is much more challenging and requires considerably more strategy than backyard croquet. The wickets are each used twice and the stake once, and the approach to the wicket comes from both directions, providing plenty of opportunity for confrontation with other balls.

The game is always played with four balls. In a singles match, two players each have two balls. In a doubles match, two players are paired up as a team, but they each have their own ball.

The stake and each wicket count as one point, giving a total of 13 points for each ball, 26 for the team. The first team to reach 26 wins.

Another difference in International Croquet is the croquet shot itself. Players are not allowed to "foot" the ball. In other words, the player still moves his ball right next to the ball that was hit, but he may not stabilize it by stepping on it. His ball is going to move too. Also, the croquet shot is not optional, as it is in the backyard game.

POISON

Number of Players: 2 to 6
Equipment: mallet and ball for each player
Playing Area: nine-wicket or six-wicket setup
Ages: 6 and up

Poison is an elimination game. It is played the same way as regular croquet—either the nine-wicket or the six-wicket—but the game isn't over at the final stake. When a player hits the stake, he is considered "poison." This means that when his ball hits another ball—even another poison ball—that ball is eliminated from the game. The winner is the person who has eliminated all of the other balls.

This game adds an extra dimension, because while there is still a race to be the first one to the post (to become the first poison), even a player who gets off to a bad start can still have a chance at winning through cagey playing.

TEAM CROQUET

Number of Players: 4 or 6
Equipment: mallet and ball for each player
Playing Area: nine-wicket setup
Ages: 6 and up

Players are divided into two teams that alternate colors on the post. A player is allowed to hit his own teammate's ball, thereby getting the extra strokes. It is often helpful for teammates to try to keep their balls together to give each other extra hits.

The object of team croquet is to get an entire team's set of balls home before the other team gets all of its balls home. Once a ball hits the stake, that ball is dead. Therefore, if a player has gone through all of the wickets, he may stop just short of hitting the final stake in order to send his opponent's balls off in the wrong direction, thereby allowing his teammates to catch up.

CROQUET

MODIFIED TEAM CROQUET

Number of Players: 2 or 3
Equipment: mallet and two or three balls for each player
Playing Area: nine-wicket setup
Ages: 8 and up

Two players may enjoy the extra challenge of Modified Team Croquet, which involves using three balls each. Three players may do this by using two balls each. Players alternate hits according to the colors on the post, just as in regular TEAM CROQUET.

While this game often involves a lot of running back and forth from both ends of the field to take care of balls in different positions, it is usually a lot more fun than regular two-person croquet because of the unpredictability of extra balls on the field.

BRITISH CROQUET

Number of Players: 2 or 3
Equipment: mallet and two or three balls for each player
Playing Area: nine-wicket or six-wicket setup
Ages: 8 and up

This is almost identical to MODIFIED TEAM CROQUET, but with one major difference. In Modified Team Croquet, players must hit the balls in the order dictated by the colors on the stake. In British Croquet, the players may choose to hit any of their balls at any time, as long as it is their turn.

For instance, if a player has the red, yellow and orange balls, for instance, he may choose to hit the red ball three turns in a row before he even touches the orange or yellow balls. Or he may want to alternate between red and orange and leave the yellow ball out of it for a while. However, he may hit only one ball per turn.

WILD WICKETS

Number of Players: 2 to 6
Equipment: mallet and ball for each player, wickets
Playing Area: field
Ages: 8 and up

One of the reasons croquet is such a great game is that it is so adaptable to playing areas, skill levels and even equipment. Wild Wickets is a game that evolved because of this very adaptability.

The starting stake is hammered into the ground, and then the wickets get divided equally among the players. Players may place their wickets anywhere on the field and in any formation that they think might benefit their skills most.

Play begins at the stake, and the first player to go decides what will be the first wicket. The first player to go through the first wicket decides what the next wicket will be and so on, until the ninth wicket. Players must then hit the starting stake to end the game. The first player who makes it back to the starting stake wins.

GOLF CROQUET

Number of Players: 2 to 6
Equipment: mallet and ball for each player, wickets
Playing Area: field
Ages: 8 and up

In golf, the player to complete the course in the fewest number of strokes is the winner. The goal is similar in Golf Croquet.

The wickets should be spread out around the playing area; they do not have to be in one of the traditional setups. The game begins as players "tee off" toward the first wicket. The player to get through the wicket first has won that wicket. Players may interfere with each other by placing their ball in the way of another player's direct shot, but there is no "sending" of another ball.

Once one player has gone through the wicket, all other players focus their attention on the next wicket. A player who has no chance of winning the current wicket may not go for the next wicket until someone has won the current wicket.

It's possible to make Golf Croquet even more like golf by varying the scoring. Instead of winning a wicket, each player must complete the entire course and count the total number of strokes. The player with the fewest is the winner.

TEAM GOLF CROQUET

Number of Players: 2 to 6
Equipment: mallet and ball for each player, wickets
Playing Area: field
Ages: 8 and up

GOLF CROQUET also can be played with teams. Players divide into two equal teams. If only two people are playing, then each person takes three balls. (Three people each take two balls.)

The rules are the same as Golf Croquet, but now a team has to get both (or all three) balls through the wicket before it can win the wicket. In a quicker version, the team has to get only one ball through to win a wicket.

5

FIELD HOCKEY

The Game

Field hockey is the oldest form of hockey. It is likely that even cavepeople batted a ball around with a stick. The game that comes closest to field hockey is a game called shinny, which was invented by the Native Americans. The rules are similar to field hockey, except that there was no limit to the number of players on each team and boundaries didn't exist.

Today's field hockey is a little more rigid, but the object remains the same—to get the ball in the opponent's goal. The team that scores the most goals is the winner. The ball is propelled along the ground by a field hockey stick. These sticks have a flat side and a rounded side, and players may use only the rounded side to hit the ball.

Each team has 11 players, usually 10 field players and a goalie. Players may not touch the ball with any part of their body, except for the flat of a hand, which may be used to stop a ball in the air as long as the ball is not directed in any manner. A goalie may kick the ball or stop it with any part of the body, but may not catch it.

To start the game, two players face off at the center of the field to gain possession of the ball or pass it to a teammate. Free hits are given when the ball goes out of bounds, when a stick is raised dangerously high, when the ball is touched by part of a player's body, when a player is offsides or when a player trips, charges or obstructs an opponent.

There are a few extra regulations depending on whether it's a men's or women's game, but these are the general rules, which are usually the same for both.

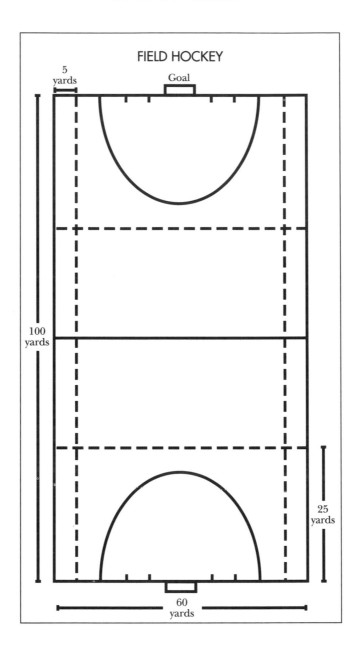

FIELD HOCKEY

5 yards

Goal

100 yards

25 yards

60 yards

PERIMETER HOCKEY

Number of Players: 8 or more
Equipment: stick for each player, ball 12 goal markers
Playing Area: circle with six goals around the perimeter
Ages: 8 and up

Perimeter Hockey works on dribbling, passing and finesse instead of the hard shot. Players divide into two teams. The team with the ball tries to get it through

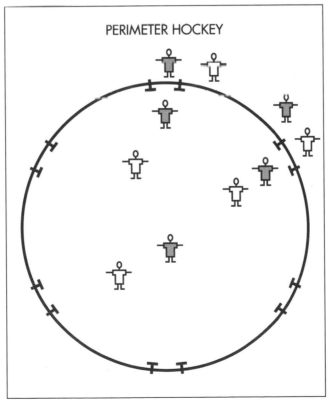

PERIMETER HOCKEY

any of the six goals, while the other team tries to stop them. At the end of the game, the team with the most goals is the winner.

The perimeter of the circle only defines where the goals are placed; it does not restrict the players in any way. In fact, in order to score a goal, a player must either dribble the ball through a goal or pass it to another player who is standing outside the goal.

If the defending team is able to get the ball away from the offensive team, then it becomes offense and tries to get a goal through the same six goals. For this reason, players should mark up man-to-man and stay very tight on their opponent at all times.

SIX-IN-A-ROW

Number of Players: 6 or more
Equipment: stick for each player, ball
Playing Area: field
Ages: 8 and up

If a player needs work on passing skills, then there is no better game than Six-in-a-Row, because there are no goals in this game, which means shooting and dribbling the ball are largely unnecessary.

The object of the game is for one team to make six consecutive passes without the other team touching the ball. Six consecutive passes equals one point. If the players are young or less experienced, three or four passes in a row will provide enough of a challenge.

FOOSEBALL

Number of Players: 12 or more
Equipment: stick for each player, ball
Playing Area: field with four zones
Ages: 8 and up

Like SIX-IN-A-ROW, Fooseball is another game in which players count passes instead of goals, but the play is slightly different. There are four zones on the field. Team A is in zones 1 and 3, and Team B is in zones 2 and 4.

The teams try to pass the ball through the opponent's zone and back again, without the opponents touching it. Every time a team is successful doing this, it scores a point. No one is allowed to leave his zone. Each team may pass within its zone as much as members want, in order to try to catch the defense out of position.

Players on a team should switch zones periodically (when play is stopped, of course) to allow everyone to play in the more challenging middle zones, where both defense and offense are important. To create more excitement, another ball can be added.

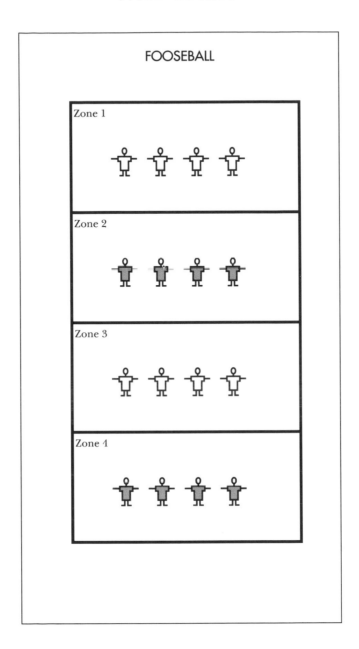

FOOSEBALL

Zone 1

Zone 2

Zone 3

Zone 4

FOUR GOALS

Number of Players: 6 or more
Equipment: stick for each player, ball
Playing Area: field with four goals marked
Ages: 8 and up

If a player is looking for shooting and defensive practice, the game of Four Goals is a good choice. This is a variation of field hockey in which each team has two goals—instead of just one—to shoot for. That means that the field,

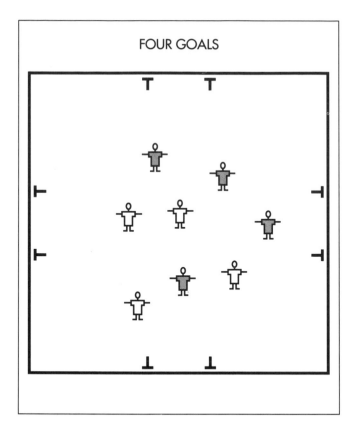

FOUR GOALS

which is generally smaller than a normal hockey field, has one goal on each of its four sides.

In addition, no goalkeepers are used, which means the goal spaces should be fairly small. Players have to mark up man-to-man, which also works to develop defensive skills, because otherwise an opponent may suddenly reverse direction and head off toward another goal. The team with the most goals at the end of the playing time wins.

PARTNERS

Number of Players: 4 or more
Equipment: stick for each player, ball
Playing area: field with four goals marked
Ages: 8 and up

This game uses the same setup as FOUR GOALS, so it's not a bad follow-up game when players feel they need a variation. Each player has a partner, which means that, depending on the number of players, there could be more than two teams on the field at once. (If there are six players, then there are three teams of two.)

The object is for a player to pass the ball through one of the goals to his partner. It can be any of the goals, and it can go through in any direction. The partner must receive it after it has gone through, however. Each time this happens, the team gets a point. The partnership with the most points at the end of the specified time wins. If there are more than six people playing, then two balls should be used.

MONKEY IN THE MIDDLE

Number of Players: 3 or more
Equipment: stick for each player, ball
Playing Area: anywhere
Ages: 8 and up

The object of this game is for two players to retain possession of the ball for as long as possible while the third player tries to get it away from them. There are no boundaries.

When the middle player finally does get control, then he switches places with the player who lost the ball in the first place. Now that person becomes the monkey in the middle.

If there are more than four players, then it is a good idea to have more than one monkey—three on two, four on two, five on two, six on three and so on. It also might be advisable to create boundaries with larger groups of players.

FIELD HOCKEY GOLF

Number of Players: 2 or more
Equipment: stick and ball for each person
Playing Area: field with cones or markers
Ages: 8 and up

Field Hockey Golf is good for developing a player's accuracy. Cones or other markers should be spread around the field, a good distance apart from each other. Players start at the first "tee" and hit the ball toward the first marker. Players keep track of how many hits it takes to get to the marker. Once both (or all) players reach the marker, the player with the fewest strokes for that "hole" chooses which marker they go after next. When all markers have been hit, the player who has completed the course in the fewest strokes is the winner.

BULL IN THE RING

Number of Players: 3 or more
Equipment: stick and ball for each person
Playing Area: small area with boundaries
Ages: 8 and up

See BULL IN THE RING (basketball).

BULLS VERSUS COWS

Number of Players: 4 or more
Equipment: sticks, balls for half the players, timer
Playing Area: small area with boundaries
Ages: 8 and up

See BULLS VERSUS COWS (basketball)

LINE HOCKEY

Number of Players: 8 or more
Equipment: stick for each person, ball
Playing Area: field with two parallel boundary lines
Ages: 8 and up

Players divide into two equal teams and stand opposite one another on the boundary lines. The teams count off so that each member of the team has a different number. For instance, if there are five players on each team, the players on each team would be numbered 1 through 5.

The referee, coach or someone who is not involved in the play calls out one or more numbers and throws the ball into the center of the field. The players whose numbers are called must rush out, retrieve the ball and try to get it across the opponent's line. Obviously, the player from the other team who has the same number will be trying to do the same thing, so it turns into a mini one-on-one game or two-on-two, and so on.

The players whose numbers are not called are left standing on the line. They may not leave the line, but they must block any attempts to get the ball over the line. Sometimes all of the numbers will be called, which leaves the line more vulnerable.

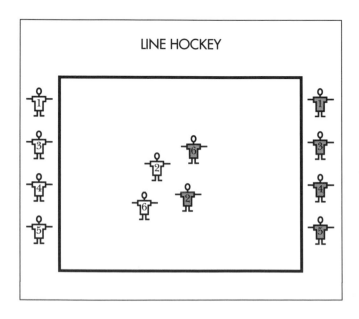

LINE HOCKEY

If a point is scored, then the players go back to their lines and the referee calls out different numbers. However, the referee may choose to do this in the middle of a play as well. If the players who are out there get their number called again, they may continue to play, but if totally new numbers are called, then they must leave the ball exactly where it is and sprint back to their line.

The winner is the team with the most points after a specified length of time.

ONE GOAL

Number of Players: 8 or more

Equipment: stick for each person, ball, two goal markers

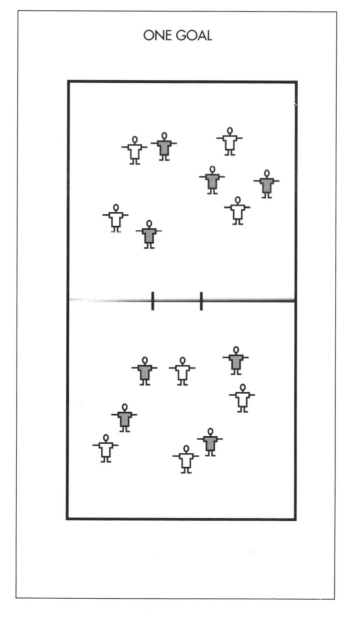

ONE GOAL

Playing Area: small field with goal in the middle
Ages: 8 and up

In this game the playing field is divided in half, with a goal set up on the center line. The goal should be approachable from both sides. Players divide into two equal teams and then divide again, so that half of each team is on each half of the field. Players may pass to their teammates on the other side of the line, but each player must stay on his own side.

The object is to score as many goals as possible, and the ball can come in from either direction. It can get very confusing because both teams are shooting for the same goal. A goal does not count unless it is clear as to which team took the shot.

HOCKEY BASEBALL

Number of Players: 8 or more
Equipment: stick for each player, ball, three cones
Playing Area: one end of field
Ages: 8 and up

Players divide into two teams, a fielding team and a batting team. Each team should have a goalie, or one goalie can play for both teams.

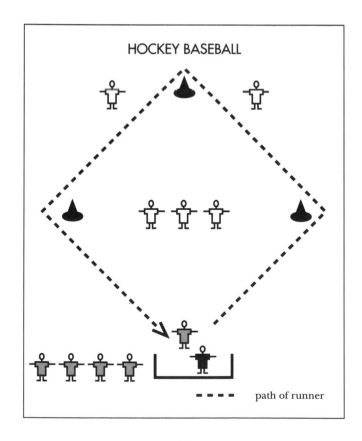

HOCKEY BASEBALL

- - - - path of runner

Three cones are set up in a baseball diamond formation, fairly far apart, with the goal being home plate. The fielders take position out in the field, the goalie (from the batting team if two goalies are playing) gets in the goal area and the "batter" steps up to the plate. The batter hits the ball somewhere out in the field and then proceeds to race around the cones. The fielders retrieve the ball and take shots on goal. If the batter gets all the way around the cones without the fielders getting a goal, then the batting team gets one run. After all of the batters have had their turn, the teams switch sides. The team with the most runs after nine innings is the winner.

FREE FOR ALL

Number of Players: 12 or more
Equipment: stick for each player, six balls
Playing Area: field
Ages: 10 and up

Free For All is a regular field hockey game, except six balls are used instead of one. Players have to keep their heads up and figure out if they want to play predominantly defensively or offensively. The rules and the scoring are the same as for field hockey.

THREE ON THREE ON THREE

Number of Players: 9 or 11 if you want to have two goalies
Equipment: stick for each player, ball
Playing Area: field
Ages: 10 and up

Three on Three on Three requires an incredible amount of running, so players who are not in shape should beware. Players form three teams of three, Team A, Team B and Team C. Team A lines up in front of one goal. Team B lines up in front of the other. Team C is in the middle. If there are goalies, then the regular goals can be used. Otherwise, the goals should be smaller.

Team C, offense, starts with the ball. Team members head down the field in the direction of Team A, defense. Team C must try to score a goal and Team A must try to stop them. When Team A gains possession of the ball, either by stealing it away from Team C or after a Team C goal is scored, members take off down the field toward Team B. Team C stays at the end where Team A was.

Team A is now offense against Team B's defense. When Team B gets possession of the ball, it takes off toward Team C. Team B is now offense; C is now defense. Play goes for a specified length of time; the team that has the most goals at the end is the winner.

DOUBLE JEOPARDY

Number of Players: 4 or more
Equipment: stick for each player, two balls

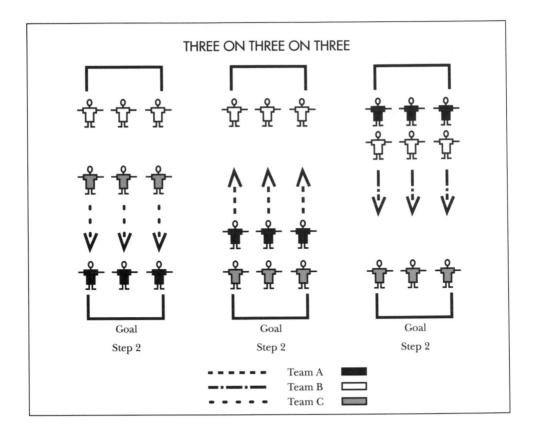

THREE ON THREE ON THREE

Goal — Step 2 | Goal — Step 2 | Goal — Step 2

Team A ▬▬▬

Team B ▭

Team C ▨

Playing Area: field with line in the middle

Ages: 8 and up

Players divide into two teams, one on each side of the line. Each team starts with a ball on its side. On cue, both teams start passing to the other side. The object is to never allow both balls to be on the same side at the same time. The team that forces its opponents to do this gets a point. Play goes to 21.

DRIBBLE AND DRIVE

Number of Players: 6 or more

Equipment: sticks, two balls

Playing Area: field with three parallel lines

Ages: 8 and up

This game is excellent for developing two skills that are essential to playing field hockey: dribbling and driving. It could almost be considered a relay race. Players divide into two teams, and then they divide in half again. The teams face each other, with half the team behind the first line and the other half behind the third line. The center line is in between them.

A coach or referee blows a whistle. The first player of each team dribbles the ball to the center line. As soon as the player reaches the center line, he drives

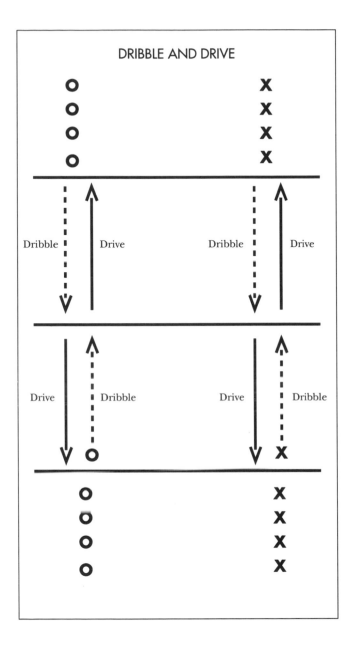

the ball toward his teammate who stands behind the third line. He then runs in the direction he passed the ball and gets in line.

The teammate standing behind the third line may either wait for the ball to come to him or go out and meet it; but if he goes out to meet it, he must then dribble it back to his line before he dribbles to the center. As indicated, he then also will dribble it to the center line and drive to the other teammate waiting behind the first line.

Play ends when all players of one team are back in their original positions. The first team to achieve this is the winner.

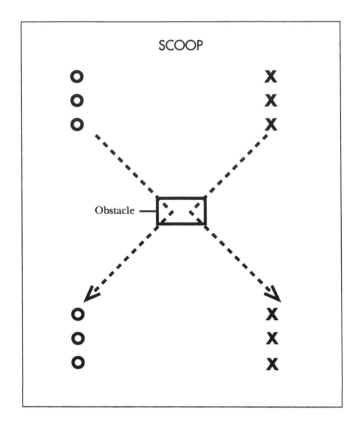

SCOOP

S C O O P

Number of Players: 6 or more
Equipment: sticks, two balls, obstacle
Playing Area: field
Ages: 10 and up

The setup of Scoop is similar to that of DRIBBLE AND DRIVE. Players divide into two equal teams and then those teams divide in half, with one half standing opposite the other a considerable distance down the field. An obstacle is placed equidistant from all four lines.

Like Dribble and Drive, this game is a race. However, the racing aspect is only one small part. At the starting whistle, the first player from each team must dribble to the center. When they near it, they must try to scoop the ball over the obstacle. If they do this successfully, they score one point for their team.

Each player gets only one try. Whether the scoop is successful or not, the player then dribbles to the teammate in the opposite line. That player takes the ball and also attempts to scoop.

The team that gets all its players back to their starting positions first gets two extra points. These are added to the scoop points, and the team with the most points is the winner.

If there are only six players, then just one point is awarded for finishing first, or speed will take precedence over the scoop. If very many people are playing, then as many as five points can be awarded.

ATTACK

Number of Players: 2 or more
Equipment: sticks, ball
Playing Area: goal
Ages: 8 and up

Players mark off three spots in front of a goal. One player is the goalie. Ideally, if there is a true goalie, then that person tends goal against the other players; otherwise players take turns being the goalie.

Players take six shots on goal, one from a standing position at each of the three spots and one each as they run toward the marked spots. Players get a point for each ball that gets past the goalie. The player with the most points after all players have taken their shots is the winner.

6

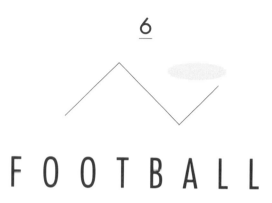

F O O T B A L L

The Game

Although football is one of the most popular sports in the United States, it really isn't played anywhere else in the world. More people place bets on the outcome of the Super Bowl, the final game in the National Football League,

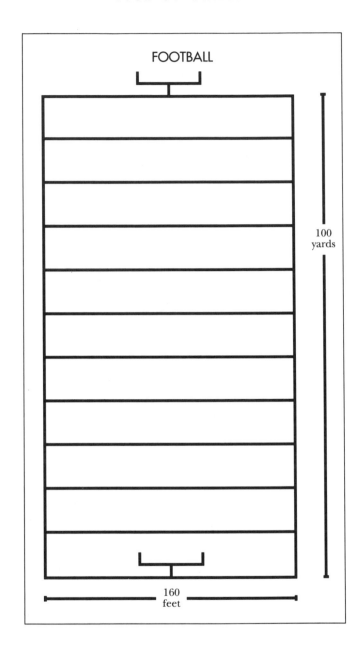

FOOTBALL

100 yards

160 feet

than any other single event, and it is usually one of the most watched television shows of the year.

The game of football evolved from the British game of rugby. In the United States, changes in the game were made gradually, and eventually the sport of football was created. The object is for one team of 11 players to move the ball over the end zone without being stopped by the opposing team of 11 players. The ball is moved down the field in three ways: passing, running and kicking.

The defensive team tries to prevent the offensive team from scoring and moving the ball down the field. Defensive players do this by tackling the player with the ball, blocking a pass or a kick, intercepting a pass or recovering a fumble. If the defensive team prevents the offensive team from moving the ball 10 yards in four tries, then it gets the ball. The offensive team often chooses to use its fourth try to punt the ball as far away from the other team's end zone as possible, because the opposing team takes its position if it fails to move the 10 yards on the fourth try.

Scoring is complicated. If a team runs or passes the ball over the end zone, it has scored a touchdown, which is worth six points. The team now is allowed to try for one extra point—by kicking the ball through the goal posts—or two extra points—by throwing or running the ball over the end zone (called a conversion). A safety is also worth two points; this happens when a team gets tackled in its own end zone. A field goal, worth three points, happens when a team uses its fourth down to kick the ball through the goal posts, rather than run or pass the ball into the end zone.

In football, play starts with a kickoff at the beginning of each half, but otherwise it starts at the line of scrimmage, where the ball was last downed. Each team puts at least seven players on either side of the line of scrimmage. Everyone else is at least one yard behind it.

The quarterback of each team can make only one forward pass per play, but all players can make as many backward passes or handoffs as they like. All players on the defensive team can intercept a pass, but the only offensive players who are eligible are those behind the scrimmage line or those at either end.

Football is a very physical game, and over the years more and more protection (such as helmets, shoulder pads, and the like) has been added for the players. This equipment must be worn if players are going to play official tackle football. Fortunately, there are many other games that provide the essence of football without the danger.

TOUCH FOOTBALL

Number of Players: 10 or more
Equipment: football
Playing Area: field with two goal lines
Ages: 8 and up

In regular football, players tackle their opponents to keep them from progressing down the field. Without proper protection and a soft field, though, this can get very dangerous—hardly a good situation for a pick-up game. Touch Football is, therefore, a good alternative.

In Touch Football, the players need only touch the opponent, but it must be with both hands. This is much less likely to cause injury and is therefore much more suited for pick-up games, where often the only equipment available is the football itself.

The rest of the rules are basically the same as regular football. Teams get four downs before the opponents get the ball. Each ball carried over the goal line is worth six points, and teams can get one point more if they complete a conversion pass.

There are some variations, however, because everywhere that Touch Football is played, people make up their own rules. Sometimes players need to touch an opponent with only one hand. Sometimes the teams allow all players to be eligible to receive passes, while others allow only a few designated players to receive. If the field is short, only three downs might be used. Some players may not bother with the conversion point. The idea is to get the most realistic, yet safe, football game that is suitable for the players and the area in which it is being played.

FLAG FOOTBALL

Number of Players: 10 or more
Equipment: football, flags for each player
Playing Area: field with two goal lines
Ages: 8 and up

Flag Football is identical to TOUCH FOOTBALL except in the way people "tackle." In Touch Football, players have to tag the ball carrier with two hands. This can often create arguments as to whether or not a player actually got both of his hands on his opponent.

In Flag Football, players carry little flags tucked into their belts. The defense must take the flag away from the ball carrier. Flags must be visible, with only one end tucked in, and they may not be tied on. The best types of flags are the commercially sold sets of Flag Football flags, which attach to a special belt with Velcro. Scoring is the same as in Touch Football.

QUARTERBACK GOLF

Number of Players: 2 or more
Equipment: football, targets
Playing Area: field
Ages: 8 and up

This is a great game for two players who each want to be the quarterback. The players set up target areas in a field or backyard. The targets should be progressively farther away from the throwing area. Players take turns receiving the snap, dropping back and throwing at the target (a can, tree, etc.). Players keep track of the number of throws it takes to hit the target. There should be a cap of six or seven, though, so that a player isn't throwing forever.

Once both players have hit the target, they move on to the next target and add that score to the first. The winner is the player with the fewest throws after all of the targets have been hit.

If keeping track of the number of throws is too difficult, there is an easy variation. Once a player has hit a target, he may move on to the next target, regardless of whether or not the other player has hit the target. A player cannot move on until he has hit the target. In this variation, the first player to hit all of the targets is the winner.

FOOTBALL

QUARTERBACK TOSS

Number of Players: 2 or more
Equipment: football for each player
Playing Area: field with targets
Ages: 8 and up

Quarterback Toss is another great game designed to help a quarterback develop his passing accuracy. Ten or 15 targets should be set up around the field. One player decides which will be the first target. The players then throw their footballs one at a time and try to hit the target. A player gets one point for each successful throw. Players take turns choosing the next target. At the end of the game, the player with the most points wins.

TARGET RUSH

Number of Players: 2 or more
Equipment: football, target
Playing Area: field
Ages: 8 and up

In Target Rush, one player is offense and one player is defense. The target and the defensive player are at one end of the field and the offensive player is at the other end. The offensive player has four downs to try to get the ball to the target.

The defensive player yells "go" to start the play. The offensive player may run with the ball or throw it at the target and try to hit it. If the defensive player tags the offensive player before he reaches the target, or the pass misses the target, then the ball is downed. Generally, the offensive player won't throw on the first down. The defensive player has a good distance to run, so the offensive player can make up some good yardage by running first.

After each down, the defensive player goes back to the target to start. After four downs, the players switch positions. The first player to hit the target 10 times is the winner.

If there are more than two players, then the defensive team can start close to the offensive team, as in regular football, because blocking can now be used to advance the ball down the field.

PASS PATTERN

Number of Players: 3
Equipment: football
Playing Area: field
Ages: 8 and up

Often it is difficult to find a game for three people because that means the teams are uneven. Pass Pattern is the perfect solution. One team consists of the quarterback and the receiver. The other team is the lone defender.

The quarterback and the receiver huddle up and figure out what pass pattern they want to run for that play. Then they run it and the defender tries to stop them. If the pass is complete, the quarterback and the receiver get one point. If it is incomplete, the defender gets one point. If the defender intercepts the ball, he gets two points. The first team to reach 21 wins.

FOURS

Number of Players: 4 or more
Equipment: football
Playing Area: field
Ages: 8 and up

In Fours, the object is for the offensive team to get as far down field as possible in four downs. Players divide into two equal teams. The offensive team is made up of a quarterback and pass receivers. The defensive team is made up of a timer and pass defenders. There is no running with the ball.

While there are no pass rushers, the quarterback must release the ball within four seconds. The timer on the defending team counts these four seconds out loud.

When the offensive team completes a pass, it moves to that position on a field, but the play still counts as one of the four downs. After the four downs, the offensive team marks the spot it reached, and the teams switch sides. The new offensive team now does the same thing. Whichever team progresses farthest gets a point for that round. The first team to get 10 points wins.

COMPLETION

Number of Players: 4 or more
Equipment: football
Playing Area: field with markers
Ages: 8 and up

Completion is a passing game in which players divide into two equal teams. The offensive team is made up of a quarterback and receivers, while the defensive team has pass defenders and one pass rusher. The pass rusher must count to three out loud before rushing, or may choose to be a pass defender instead.

In order to score points, a pass must be completed. Markers (T-shirts, cones, or chalk lines) should be placed at three different intervals down the field. It's worth one point if the pass is completed after the first marker, two points after the second, and three points after the third. An incomplete pass is worth zero.

The offensive team secretly decides which pass it is going to try for or, if there are several pass receivers, they can all go out at different lengths and the quarterback can decide. After each pass, the offensive and defensive teams trade places. The first team to reach 21 wins.

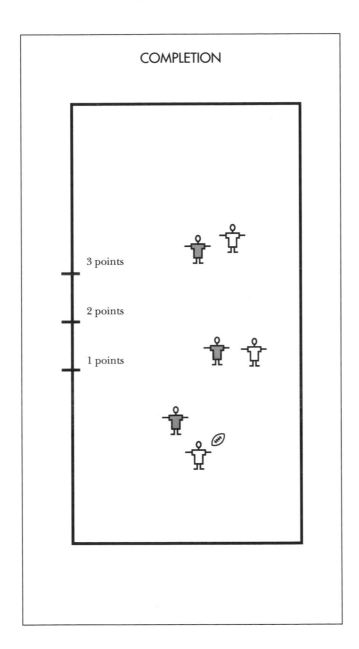

COMPLETION

3 points

2 points

1 points

BLOCK OUT

Number of Players: 2 or more
Equipment: football, chalk (or masking tape)
Playing Area: wall
Ages: 8 and up

Block Out is another great game for two aspiring quarterbacks. This game is played against a wall. The players should draw six targets on the wall with chalk (or masking tape). Inside each target is written a number from one to six;

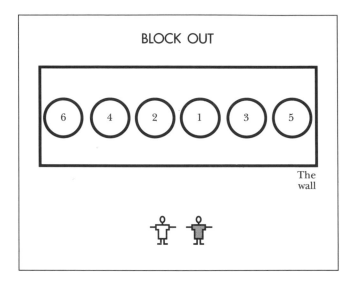

these are the points. The object of the game is to hit the targets and get the most points.

Getting points is somewhat complicated, however. A player must hit a target three times before he can get any points for it. Every time he hits it after that, he gets the number of points inside the target, provided the other player has not yet hit that same target three times.

Once both players have hit a target three times, the target is "blocked out"—no one can get any more points from it. In other words, only one player can get points from a specific target; and sometimes it happens that no one gets points for a particular target. The game is over when all six targets are blocked out.

The best way to keep track of the score is with a piece of chalk on the pavement or with a stick in the ground. Otherwise, trying to remember the score and who has hit which target how many times is close to impossible. The player with the most points wins.

KICKER GOLF

Number of Players: 2 or more
Equipment: football
Playing Area: field with marked spots and goal post
Ages: 8 and up

For Kicker Golf, the players set up kicking spots on the field. These spots should be varied—close, far away and at different angles. The players start at one of these spots and alternate kicking for a field goal, while the other player holds the ball. They keep track of the number of attempts it takes for them to get one.

Once both players have gotten a field goal from one spot, they move to the next spot and add that score to the first. The winner is the player with the fewest number of attempts after all of the spots have been tried.

FOOTBALL

AROUND THE WORLD

Number of Players: 2 or more
Equipment: football
Playing Area: field with marked spots and goal post
Ages: 8 and up

Like KICKER GOLF, Around the World uses spots marked on the field; but these spots should form a big arc surrounding the goal post. Six to eight spots is usually a good number.

The game starts at the spot on the end, where the first player goes for a field goal. If the field goal is good, he goes on to the next spot and kicks a field goal from there.

If the kick misses, however, then the player can take a chance kick. If the chance kick goes in, the player continues on to the next marked spot as before. If, on the other hand, the chance kick misses, the player's turn is over and he must start from the beginning on the next turn. A chance kick can be declined, however, which means the player remains at the achieved spot, but it will be the end of his turn. The game ends when one person gets all of the way around the arc.

There are a few variations to this game: It can be played without the chance kick; and it can be played with two chance kicks, with the first miss sending the player back only one spot and the second sending the player back to the beginning. The more creative the players, the more fun Around the World can be.

KICK RETURN

Number of Players: 2 or more
Equipment: football, kicker's tee
Playing Area: field
Ages: 8 and up

To start Kick Return, the football should be set up in a kicker's tee. One person is the kicker and the other is the receiver. The receiver goes toward the end of the field, and then the kicker kicks the ball.

The receiver catches the ball and tries to run with it past the tee. The kicker tries to stop him with a two-hand touch or a tackle. If the receiver passes the tee, then he gets a point. Players switch positions after each kick. The first player to reach seven points is the winner.

If there are more than two players, then they are divided into two equal teams. The person who is not receiving the ball is a blocker, and the person who is not kicking the ball helps the kicker tackle.

PASS RETURN

Number of Players: 2 or more
Equipment: football
Playing Area: field
Ages: 8 and up

Pass Return is an almost identical game to KICK RETURN, but the ball is passed instead of kicked. The passer throws to the receiver from the end zone. It is the receiver's job to catch the ball and get back into the end zone without being tackled by the passer.

Also as in Kick Return, the first player to reach seven points is the winner. More players can be added without changing the game.

SHUTTLE

Number of Players: 4 or more
Equipment: football
Playing Area: field
Ages: 6 and up

Shuttle is a good game for beginners. More experienced players will find it too easy. Players divide into two equal teams and the teams stand opposite each other, far enough apart to provide a challenge. The players line up one behind the other.

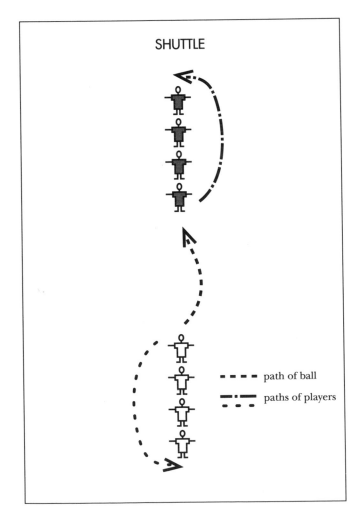

SHUTTLE

- - - - path of ball
—·—·— paths of players

The first player from one line throws the football to the first player in the opposite line. Then he runs to the end of his line. The first player in the receiving line catches the ball and throws it back to the first line, where there is now a new front person.

Play continues like this until someone misses a catch. That player is then eliminated. The first team to have all of its players eliminated loses.

SOLO SHUTTLE

Number of Players: 6 or more
Equipment: football
Playing Area: field
Ages: 8 and up

See SOLO SHUTTLE (badminton).

ASSOCIATION FOOTBALL

Number of Players: 4 or more
Equipment: football
Playing Area: field with two goal areas
Ages: 10 and up

Players divide into two equal teams and line up in each of the goal areas. The team with the ball throws or kicks the ball down the field to the other team. Both teams then chase after it, but the receiving team must touch the ball first.

The object of the game is to get the ball over the other team's goal line, either by running or passing an unlimited number of times. The other team tries to stop this. If a player with the ball is tagged, then it counts as a down. If a passed ball is dropped, it is also a down. A team is allowed four downs before the other team gains possession.

One point is scored for each ball over the goal line, and a new kick-off is set up. The first team to score 15 points is the winner.

SMEAR

Number of Players: 3 or more
Equipment: football
Playing Area: field
Ages: 5 and up

Smear can be found on nearly every elementary school playground and is probably one of the best known and most violent versions of football. It's very simple. The player who has the football is tackled (sometimes piled on) by everyone else. To avoid this, he runs away or tosses the ball to another player. Then everyone chases after the new person. There are no winners.

KEEP AWAY

Number of Players: 4 or more
Equipment: football
Playing Area: field
Ages: 5 and up

Keep Away is a slightly more civilized version of SMEAR. In this game there are actually teams and an achievable goal. Still, the animalistic playground atmosphere is very prominent.

The object of the game is for one team to hold onto the ball as long as possible. If a player is tackled, then the other team gets the ball; before a player is close to being tackled, he attempts to dish the ball off to one of his teammates. The other team also may gain control of the ball through an interception or a fumble. There are no points or winners in this game.

ANIMAL BALL

Number of Players: 3 or 4
Equipment: football
Playing Area: field
Ages: 6 and up

Animal Ball is an equally brutal game, but this one is quite different from SMEAR and KEEP AWAY. In Animal Ball, one player is the quarterback and the others are receivers. The quarterback calls out a play and the receivers take off for that spot. The quarterback throws the ball and the receivers battle each other to catch it. Whoever catches the ball gets to be quarterback next. If no one catches it, the same quarterback throws again.

SNOW FOOTBALL

Number of Players: 4 or more
Equipment: football
Playing Area: field covered in deep snow
Ages: 8 and up

Except for the weather conditions, Snow Football doesn't vary much from regular football. In fact, many of the games in this chapter could be adapted to Snow Football conditions. Surprisingly, it's a popular way to play football in the northern states.

With deep snow and all of the extra clothes that are necessary to be outside in the winter (jacket, gloves, hat, and so on), tackling is considerably less painful, which means that players can simulate more of a real football game than in TOUCH FOOTBALL and FLAG FOOTBALL. Also, the snow is quite a hindrance to anyone who is trying to sprint down the field. It can be a rather funny game.

FOOTBALL

ROLLBALL

Number of Players: 1
Equipment: football, soccer ball
Playing Area: field
Ages: 10 and up

In football, quarterbacks like to lead the running receiver so that the pass will land in his hands without forcing him to break stride. It's easy to practice this if there's another person around, but sometimes there isn't. That's where Rollball can be a helpful game to play.

The soccer ball (or volleyball or basketball) is now the receiver. The player rolls or kicks the ball down the field and then tries to throw the football so that it lands on—or right in front of—the moving soccer ball. The player should set a goal—for example, 10 hits—and see how many attempts it takes to achieve that goal.

BULLETBALL

Number of Players: 8 or more
Equipment: football
Playing Area: field
Ages: 10 and up

If you crossed football with ULTIMATE FRISBEE, you'd have Bulletball. This is a game that removes all of the kicking and some of the running of regular football. You can play it tackle, touch or flag.

Players take the usual positions on the field. Any play forward of the scrimmage line must always be set in motion with a pass. A player can run with the ball only after a pass has been caught. Players can continue to pass any time.

Touchdowns, worth one point each, are the only way to score. If the game is being played on a football field with goal posts, then a touchdown that happens between the goal posts can be worth two points, just to add an extra dimension.

F R I S B E E

The Game

The sport of Frisbee was born in the early 1900s when William Russell Frisbie created the Frisbie Pie Company in New Haven, Connecticut. Apparently, the pie tins and cookie lids were ideal for tossing, once the baked goods were eaten. These pie tin games spread to college campuses and military bases all over the country. The design was patented in the United States by Fred Morrison in 1948. Eventually, Wham-O recognized the popularity of Frisbie tin throwing and in 1958 created a plastic disc called a Frisbee specifically for the sport.

The invention of the Frisbee opened up a whole new realm in the sports world. Aside from creating new game possibilities, the simple act of throwing and catching a Frisbee has become an art form.

ULTIMATE FRISBEE

Number of Players: 4 or more (officially 14)
Equipment: Frisbee
Playing Area: field
Ages: 8 and up

The playing area in Ultimate Frisbee should have two end zones, just as in football. The object of the game is to pass the Frisbee to a teammate in the end zone for a point. The team with the most points at the end of the game is the winner.

Each team stands behind its own goal line. The team with the Frisbee throws it toward the receiving team and the game begins. When a person has the Frisbee in his possession, he must remain in that spot. He may pivot on one foot, however,

to avoid the defense and make a throw. Once he has thrown the Frisbee to a teammate, he should run ahead to be available for the next pass. The Frisbee must always be thrown, never handed to someone.

If the Frisbee is intercepted, hits the ground or goes out of bounds before the player's teammate catches it, then the other team has possession.

FRISBEE TENNIS

Number of Players: 2
Equipment: Frisbee
Playing Area: tennis court
Ages: 8 and up

Frisbee Tennis is the game of tennis played with a Frisbee instead of rackets and a ball. Players take their positions opposite each other on either side of the court. The serving player tosses the Frisbee, which if it landed, would come to rest in the correct service box.

However, the opposing player must catch the Frisbee in the air; otherwise, if it lands in bounds, the serving player receives a point. When the receiving player catches the Frisbee, he sends it back, and a rally has begun. The players toss the Frisbee back and forth.

If, at any point, the receiving player thinks that the Frisbee will not land within the court (or in the service box on a serve), then he may choose not to catch it and allow it to sail out of bounds, thus giving him the point. Scoring is the same as in tennis.

FRISBEE

DOUBLE DISC

Number of Players: 4
Equipment: two Frisbees
Playing Area: tennis court
Ages: 8 and up

One might think this would be like FRISBEE TENNIS, but the only thing these two games have in common is the playing area, a tennis court. Double Disc is a doubles game, however, which requires two Frisbees.

Each team starts with a Frisbee on its side. On cue, each side throws the Frisbee to the other side. The object is never to allow both discs to be on the same side at the same time. The team that manages to send both Frisbees to the opponents' side gets a point. Play goes to 21.

Obviously, there is a distinct advantage to rushing the net in order to grab the Frisbee quickly and send it back; but if it is returned to the back court, it will be difficult to get to, which almost guarantees that both Frisbees will end up on one side.

FRISBEE GOLF

Number of Players: 2 or more
Equipment: Frisbee for each player
Playing Area: golf course or area with designated "holes"
Ages: 8 and up

Frisbee Golf is called Folf in some parts of the country. The object of this game is to throw the Frisbee from hole to hole using as few tosses as possible. The player with the fewest tosses at the end of the course is the winner, just as in regular golf. If the game is played on an actual golf course, the Frisbee obviously does not go into the hole, but it must hit the flag.

During the 1970s, Frisbee Golf was so big that many parks set up official Frisbee Golf courses for it. These were complete with score cards, teeing-off areas and wire baskets (the holes). Some even had tournaments.

The craze has subsided, however, and these days most Frisbee Golf courses are informal ones. Many college campuses have courses "set up" using, for example, a sculpture for the first hole, a large flowerpot for the second hole, the peak of an archway for the third, the window of the dean's office for the fourth and so on. These courses are often passed on by word of mouth and are surprisingly consistent over the years, but the beauty of Frisbee Golf is that it can be played almost anywhere.

FRISBEE BASEBALL

Number of Players: 8 or more
Equipment: Frisbee
Playing Area: baseball field
Ages: 10 and up

Not surprisingly, Frisbee Baseball—also called Basebee—is played almost like regular baseball. Players divide into two equal teams, a fielding team and a batting team. There is no pitcher on the fielding team, although if there are a lot of players, someone may want to stand in that position for fielding purposes.

The "batter" steps up to the plate and tosses the Frisbee somewhere into the field. He then takes off for first base. Even if the Frisbee is caught in the air, it does not count as an out. The only way to get an out is to get the Frisbee to the base before the runner gets there. After three outs, the teams switch sides. The team with the most runs after nine innings is the winner.

GUTS

Number of Players: 2 or more (best with 10)
Equipment: Frisbee
Playing Area: anywhere
Ages: 8 and up

Players divide into two equal teams, and although it can be played with any number, the official game is played five on five. The goal area is the width of the players when their arms are outstretched, and the height is the height of the players' arms when they are upright.

The object of the game is for a team to deliver a good, hard throw into the goal space, so that the opposing team is unable to catch it cleanly. A clean catch is defined as a catch using only one hand and no other part of the body. A good throw that is not caught cleanly counts as one point for the throwers. A throw that is outside the goal space counts as one point for the receivers. The first team to reach 21 wins.

The player who catches or touches the Frisbee returns the throw. If nobody touches it because it is a bad throw, then any player may return the Frisbee.

TOSS AND CATCH

Number of Players: 1
Equipment: Frisbee
Playing Area: anywhere
Ages: 8 and up

This is a good solo game, but it should be played when there is a strong wind. The idea is to throw the Frisbee across the wind, to allow for maximum loft. This gives the tosser enough time to sprint and catch his own throw. Players should try to increase their distance every time. There are professional competitions for this particular skill.

SHUTTLE

Number of Players: 4 or more
Equipment: Frisbee

FRISBEE

Playing Area: field
Ages: 8 and up

See SHUTTLE (football).

SOLO SHUTTLE

Number of Players: 6 or more
Equipment: Frisbee
Playing Area: field
Ages: 8 and up

See SOLO SHUTTLE (badminton).

CIRCLE FRISBEE

Number of Players: 3 or more
Equipment: Frisbee
Playing Area: field
Ages: 8 and up

This is a simple elimination game. Players stand in a circle as large or as small as they want to make it. Traditionally, only one Frisbee is used, but if there are a lot of players, more can be added. Players toss the Frisbee to anyone in the circle. This person must catch it and send it to someone else. If a player misses the Frisbee or makes an uncatchable throw, he is eliminated. The last player in the circle is the winner.

8

GOLF

The Game

Most people believe that the game of golf was invented in Scotland, although there is evidence that a similar game—paganica—was played by the Romans. The Netherlands also is a potential location of golf's origins. The game of kolven is very similar to golf, and many words, such as "tee" and "putt," come from Dutch words for those golf terms. Early Dutch drawings show putters addressing a hole and other players teeing off.

Nonetheless, Scotland does deserve some credit for golf. The country has produced some of the world's most challenging and beautiful golf courses, and there are references to the game throughout Scottish history. It has become a national pastime, and its popularity there has helped spread it to the rest of the world.

Generally, golf is played on an 18-hole course. Each hole is usually between 200 and 600 yards long, which leads up to the green—a long grassy area with a three-inch-diameter hole at the end. The players move the golf ball from the "tee" toward the hole by hitting it with a variety of golf clubs. The player who makes it through all 18 holes in the fewest strokes is the winner. This is called stroke play, and it is the traditional way to play golf.

MATCH PLAY GOLF

Number of Players: 2 or more
Equipment: clubs and golf balls
Playing Area: golf course
Ages: 8 and up

Early golf used to be Match Play Golf, and many people still play this way for variety. This method scores the games by holes rather than strokes. The player who has the fewest number of strokes on a particular hole wins that hole. The winner is the player who wins the most holes.

Match Play Golf allows a golfer to recover after a particularly bad hole, but the downside is that games are often decided long before 18 holes have been played.

FLOG

Number of Players: 2 or more
Equipment: clubs, golf balls
Playing Area: golf course
Ages: 10 and up

The object of Flog is the opposite of golf (hence the reversed-spelling name), in that you want to get as many points as possible.

There are six different ways to get points. The easiest way is to win the hole. (That ensures that there will be at least 18 points for the course.) A player gets another point for a birdie (one stroke under par—the required amount of strokes for a given hole), even though he will probably get a point for winning the hole anyway.

The next few ways to get points are a little more untraditional, rewarding good and bad play at the same time. A woodie is when a player hits a tree on his way to the green, yet still gets par. The next is a sandie, which happens when a player lands in a sand trap and still gets par. A greenie is when the player gets to the green on one stroke, yet still pars a hole. The last one is the arnie, which is given to any player who gets to the green without once being on the fairway and still gets par. A player gets one point for each of these.

Flog is really only a game for good golfers, though, because inexperienced golfers will rarely hit a tree or a sand trap and still get par.

DEFENDER

Number of Players: 3
Equipment: clubs, golf balls
Playing Area: golf course
Ages: 10 and up

Defender adds yet another way to score in golf, and it's the perfect game to play if there is only a threesome instead of the traditional four players.

On each hole, one person is the defender and the other two are challengers. The challengers work as a team, and one of them has to beat the defender on that particular hole. If this happens, each challenger gets one dot (or point) apiece. If the defender beats or ties both of the challengers, he gets two dots on that hole. Players also can pick up two extra dots by getting a birdie on a hole.

The positions rotate on each hole. Because there are 18 holes, each player is the defender six times. The player with the most dots at the end of the 18 holes is the winner.

SANDIE

Number of Players: 3
Equipment: clubs, golf balls
Playing Area: golf course
Ages: 10 and up

Sandie is the game of DEFENDER with an added twist. Players get a dot the same way as in Defender, but now they also can get one by making a sandie.

A sandie involves getting out of the sand trap and into the hole in two shots or less. The scoring gets complicated, however. The first sandie opportunity of a match is worth one dot if the player makes it; the next sandie opportunity is also worth one dot. However, if the person going for the first sandie fails, the next sandie opportunity is worth two dots. The dot award goes up by one with every failed sandie opportunity until someone successfully makes a sandie. When this happens, the dot award for the next sandie returns to one.

The player with the most total dots at the end of the 18 holes is the winner.

SPEED GOLF

Number of Players: 2 or more
Equipment: clubs and golf balls
Playing Area: golf course
Ages: 8 and up

In Speed Golf, the score doesn't matter; the object of the game is to get through the course as fast as possible. In an indirect way, however, it is still important to get the ball in the hole in as few strokes as possible, because each stroke takes up more time.

Players must wait for the ball to come to a complete rest before they can hit it again. The player to complete the course in the shortest amount of time—regardless of score—is the winner.

BEST BALL

Number of Players: 4 or more
Equipment: clubs and golf balls
Playing Area: golf course
Ages: 8 and up

THE SPEED GOLF CHAMP

A Speed Golf player named James Carvill holds the world record for the fastest game of golf. On June 18, 1987 he played the 18-hole course at Warrenpoint Golf Club in County Down, Northern Ireland in 27 minutes and 9 seconds.[1] ○

93

Best Ball is a team game, so one player can have an off day and still be able to win. The game is played like regular golf. On each hole, the player with the best score on one team compares his score with the best score of the other team. Whichever team has the lower score gets one point for that hole.

This game also can be played with large groups of golfers. Each foursome can be a team, and when the 18 holes are finished, the scorecards are compared to find out which foursome won the most holes.

CAPTAIN AND CREW

Number of Players: 8 or more
Equipment: clubs and golf balls
Playing Area: golf course
Ages: 8 and up

Captain and Crew is also called Scramble in some areas of the country. It is a great way for a large group to play golf and is used in some tournaments, especially where the skill levels vary.

A team, usually a foursome, plays together. To begin, all team members drive off the first tee. The members then select the drive they think is the best of the four; all other members pick up their drives and hit their second stroke from the chosen spot. Again, team members look at the best second shot and drop their balls there. This continues until one of their balls goes in the hole. They count the good strokes, which becomes the total score for that hole. At the end of the course, the foursome with the fewest strokes is the winner.

There are a couple of fun variations to this game too. On one designated hole, all members are instructed to use only their five iron for every stroke, including driving and putting. Another variation requires that at some point during the 18 holes, each player must contribute two drives to the team's effort. This creates some interesting strategy decisions, especially if one player is considerably worse than the others.

HORSESHOE GOLF

Number of Players: 2 or more
Equipment: clubs, golf balls
Playing Area: golf course
Ages: 8 and up

Horseshoe Golf is played without a putter, because the ball never has to go into the hole. Players drive and chip just as in regular golf, but as soon as a player is on the green, his play on that hole is over.

Once all of the players are on the green, the person who has hit the ball closest to the hole receives one point. Play then moves to the next tee. The player with the most points at the end of the game is the winner.

The number of strokes does not matter in this game, so sometimes it is more advantageous for a player to take a few extra strokes on the fairway in order to put himself in a good position to chip onto the green.

SNEAKER GOLF

In what might be considered another version of Foot Golf, students at Williams College in Williamstown, Massachusetts used to play Sneaker Golf after dinner on the way back to the dorm. Each player would take off one sneaker. Someone would designate a "hole"—for example, the third column from the left on Chapin Hall—and the players would all throw their sneaker toward that "hole." The player to hit the "hole" with his sneaker on the least number of attempts won that hole and got to choose the next one. There is no ball. The sneaker is the ball. Except for the fact that Williamstown has snow on the ground for six months out of the year, the game was a big success. ○

FOOT GOLF

Number of Players: 2 or more
Equipment: tennis ball for each player
Playing Area: golf course
Ages: 8 and up

Foot Golf is the perfect game for people who find themselves on a beautiful golf course without any golf equipment to play it. However, very few courses would allow this game to be played, due to potential damage it could cause to the grounds.

For Foot Golf, all you need is a tennis ball. Players "tee off" from the tee area by kicking the tennis ball as far as they can. Any manner of kicking is acceptable, but the ball is not to be touched by the hands.

Play continues as in regular golf, and the ball must go into the hole. The player with the fewest number of kicks by the end of the course is the winner.

MINIATURE GOLF

Number of Players: 2 or more
Equipment: putter and ball for each player
Playing Area: miniature golf course
Ages: 4 and up

As a highly popular "family activity" rather than "sport," thousands of Miniature Golf courses can be found all over the country. The game obviously earned the name Miniature Golf because the course is significantly smaller than a regular course. In fact, only putting is involved. To make the game more interesting, these courses consist of blockades, angles, turns and hills to prevent the golf ball from reaching the hole. Players count the number of strokes it takes to complete the course, and the player with the fewest is the winner.

Miniature Golf also can be homemade. In the backyard, people can set up tin cans as holes. These homemade courses often are more challenging than the

CREATION OF MINIATURE GOLF

The credit for Miniature Golf is generally given to a Tennessee hotel owner named Garnet Carter. He built a small course that he called Fairyland to attract more people to his hotel and regular golf course. Soon Fairyland became the most popular part of the whole resort.[2]

readymade Miniature Golf because chipping and lofted shots also can be incorporated. Also, the grass will probably be much longer than the closely cropped golf greens (or Astroturf) of commercial miniature golf, which will make putting a lot more difficult.

DRIVING RANGE TARGET

Number of Players: 2
Equipment: golf balls
Playing Area: driving range
Ages: 10 and up

When most people go to the driving range, they work primarily on getting some good distance out of the ball. Achieving distance is an important part of golf, yet accuracy in distance shots is just as crucial, and that's where this game comes in.

Usually driving ranges have distance markers along them. In this game, these markers will serve as the targets. Each player gets two shots at each target; the player who comes closest gets a point. Then players aim for the next distance marker. The first player to reach 10 points wins that round.

Players should practice using several different clubs to get the right amount of loft and distance on their ball. This couldn't be a more perfect way to develop skills on a driving range.

ANGEL, DEVIL

Number of Players: 1
Equipment: clubs, two balls of different colors
Playing Area: golf course
Ages: 10 and up

Angel, Devil is a great game for anyone who has ever felt slightly schizophrenic or for anyone who wants to play golf and can't find a partner.

The game is played like regular golf, except that the player has to hit two balls on every hole. One colored ball, the angel, represents the player's good side. The other colored ball is the player's devilish side. The player should keep track of which ball does the best through the 18 holes. The ball with the lowest score at the end indicates which side of the player is dominant that day. It's a great game for solo entertainment, and it provides a rewarding psychiatric analysis too.

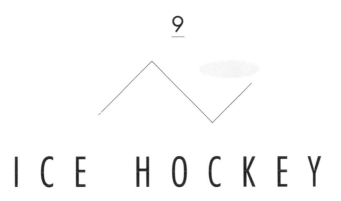

9

ICE HOCKEY

The Game

No one is exactly sure how ice hockey started, but the theory holds that it was invented in Canada when people tried to play cricket during icy winters. Of course, field hockey was around for centuries before this, and it seems the likely precursor to ice hockey.

Ice hockey consists of six players per team—three forwards, two wings and a goalie. The object of the game is to use a hockey stick to propel the puck into the goal. The team that scores the most goals is the winner. The goalie is the only player who may use his hands (unless a player needs to knock down a flying puck). The puck must be kept in motion at all times.

Game begins with a face-off in the center circle. Other face-offs occur only if play is stopped (such as when a puck goes out of bounds). Players pass, shoot and skate with the puck in an effort to get by the defense and put the puck in the goal.

A few rules are peculiar to ice hockey. There are five lines on the ice, beginning with two goal lines. The goal-tending net is set on the goal line, but players may go over this line (and behind the goal) to keep the puck in play. Next is the red line, which is in the center of the ice. Players who are behind the red line may not shoot the puck across the goal line. This offense is called icing. The only time it is a legal shot is when the puck goes in the goal.

There are also two blue lines. No attacker can cross the blue line in the attacking zone ahead of the puck. If he does, it is called offsides. If the puck goes out of the zone and an attacking player hits it back in before his teammate has had a chance to get out, the player is not offsides unless he touches the puck. He

may skate across the blue line and back into the zone, and then he is able to touch the puck.

A number of fouls can be called, which supposedly prevent roughness. There is no kneeing or elbowing, no high sticks, no tripping, no spearing (with the stick), no board checking, no hooking (trying to stop a player by forcing the stick around his body), no holding, no kicking and no fighting. These are actual rules, although anyone watching the professional games on television might wonder to what extent they're ever enforced. Fortunately, protective gear is warn.

ICING

Number of Players: 2 or more
Equipment: stick and two pucks for each player
Playing Area: ice with a finish line clearly marked
Ages: 6 and up

Icing is a race, but it develops accuracy and control as well as speed. Players each have two pucks. If possible, one of the two pucks should have a red or white dot on it to distinguish it from the other.

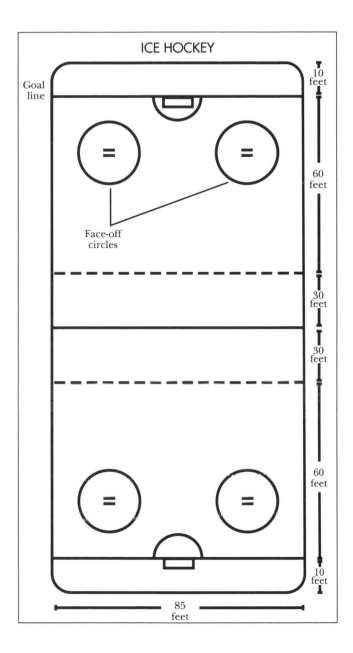

The marked puck is the target. It is placed five to 10 feet beyond the starting line, depending on the skill levels of the players. At the signal, each player begins by shooting his puck at his respective target puck, in an effort to move it closer to the finish line.

A player has to consider the trade-off. If he hits his puck hard, it will send his target puck farther than if he hits it gently. However, there is also a good chance that he will miss his target puck; and if the puck is hit too hard, then the players will have to skate after it and bring it all of the way back, wasting quite a bit of time.

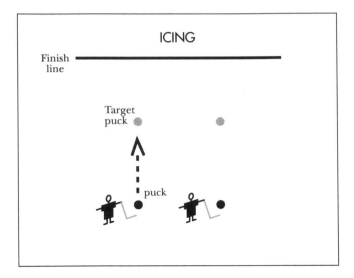

A player is not allowed to touch his target puck with his stick. If he does, he must go all the way back to the starting line. The first player to get his target puck over the finish line wins.

SLAPSHOT

Number of Players: 2
Equipment: sticks for each player, puck
Playing Area: ice with goal area
Ages: 6 and up

Slapshot is perhaps the most basic hockey game in existence, yet kids play it constantly. One player is the goalie, while the other player is the shooter. The shooter has 10 attempts to fire a slapshot past the goalie. Then the players switch positions, with the other player now having 10 shots. The first player to achieve 21 slapshot goals is the winner. It's a good idea to create a line at least five feet away that limits how close a shooter may skate, or the game could get dangerous.

PINSHOT

Number of Players: 4 or more
Equipment: stick for each player, puck, 8 or 10 bowling pins
Playing Area: ice
Ages: 8 and up

Pinshot is a regular hockey game without goals and goalkeepers. Instead, four or five bowling pins are set up at each end of the rink, spaced a good distance apart from each other. Players divide into two equal teams and then play hockey. The first team to knock down all of its opponents' pins with the puck is the

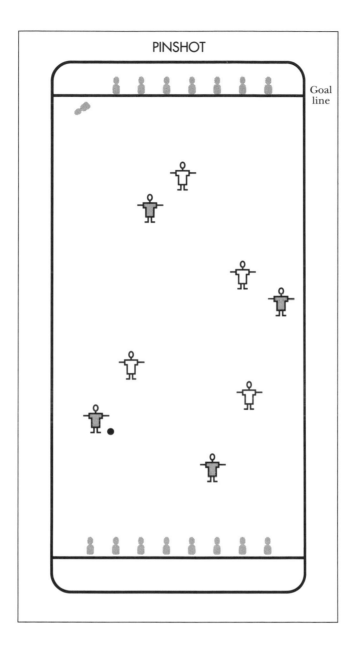

PINSHOT

Goal
line

winner. If a player knocks down a pin with something other than the puck, he must set the pin back up, and the other team gets a free shot.

FOUR GOALS

Number of Players: 6 or more
Equipment: stick for each player, puck
Playing Area: ice with four goals
Ages: 8 and up

See FOUR GOALS (field hockey).

SIX-IN-A-ROW

Number of Players: 6 or more
Equipment: stick for each player, puck
Playing Area: ice
Ages: 8 and up

See SIX-IN-A-ROW (field hockey).

FOOSEBALL

Number of Players: 12 or more
Equipment: stick for each player, puck
Playing Area: ice with four zones marked
Ages: 8 and up

See FOOSEBALL (field hockey).

THREE ON GOAL

Number of Players: 4
Equipment: stick for each player, puck, cone

Playing Area: ice with cone in the center
Ages: 8 and up

The object of Three on Goal is twofold. Three players are the shooters, who want to keep the puck away from the fourth player and also to score by hitting the cone with the puck. The fourth player is the goalie; he defends the cone from the puck.

The shooters get a point each time they hit the cone. The goalie gets a point each time he touches the puck, which means that the shooters have to be judicious in choosing their shots. They don't want to just fire the puck randomly. Because the shooters can hit the cone from all sides, however, with quick passing and skating, they may be able to catch the goalie on the wrong side of the cone and get a shot off. The first player to reach 10 points is the winner.

DOUBLE JEOPARDY

Number of Players: 4 or more
Equipment: stick for each player, two pucks
Playing Area: ice with line in the middle
Ages: 8 and up

See DOUBLE JEOPARDY (field hockey)

LINE HOCKEY

Number of Players: 8 or more
Equipment: stick for each player, puck
Playing Area: ice with two parallel boundary lines
Ages: 8 and up

See LINE HOCKEY (field hockey).

ONE GOAL

Number of Players: 8 or more
Equipment: stick for each player, puck, two goal markers
Playing Area: ice with goal in the middle
Ages: 8 and up

See ONE GOAL (field hockey).

DUCK

Number of Players: 8 or more
Equipment: puck and stick for each player
Playing Area: rink
Ages: 6 and up

See DUCK (basketball).

STREET HOCKEY

Number of Players: 6 or more
Equipment: stick for each player, tennis ball or rubber ball
Playing Area: street with goals
Ages: 6 and up

Street Hockey is a game that can be played in the off-season. Players wear sneakers instead of ice skates, and a ball is used instead of a puck. Players defend, pass and shoot just as in ice hockey. Play is almost identical, although some of the finer ice hockey rules are overlooked in Street Hockey pick-up games.

BROOMBALL

Number of Players: 6 or more
Equipment: broom for each player, rubber playground ball
Playing Area: ice
Ages: 6 and up

Broomball is a combination of STREET HOCKEY and ice hockey. It's played on ice with ice hockey rules, but players wear sneakers and bat a ball around instead of a puck. The sticks are usually brooms, but if there is a shortage of brooms, players can use regular hockey sticks. The challenge of the game comes less from hockey skills than from the ability to stay upright when racing across ice in sneakers.

THREE ON THREE ON THREE

Number of Players: 9 or 11 if you want to have two goalies
Equipment: stick for each player, ball
Playing Area: ice
Ages: 8 and up

See THREE ON THREE ON THREE (field hockey).

10

LACROSSE

The Game

It is generally acknowledged that the game of lacrosse was invented by Native Americans. Any number of men could play—often numbering into the hundreds—and the games could go on for several hours. They had goals but no boundaries.

THE SWALLOWING-THE-BALL TRICK

When Native Americans first developed lacrosse, there was no standard size for the ball. Players would use whatever someone had made. Generally, though, the ball was much smaller than it is today. Because the ball was smaller, occasionally a player would hide it in his mouth as he ran toward the goal. Obviously, a rule was quickly added to prevent this from occurring.[3]   ○

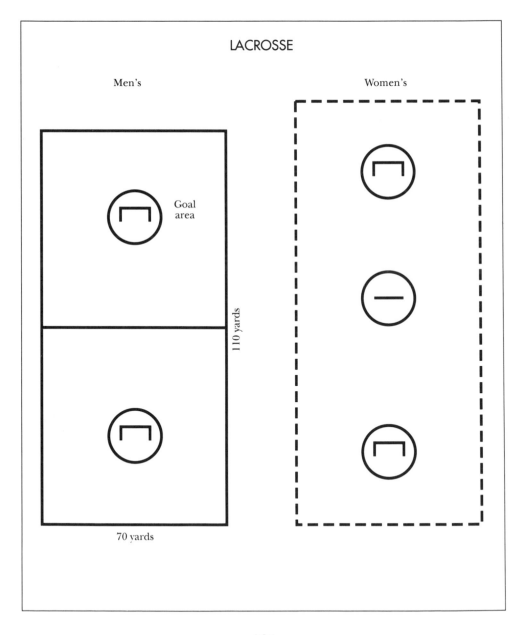

LACROSSE

The rules of lacrosse vary depending on whether men or women are playing. Women's lacrosse, for instance, has no boundaries, whereas the men's game does. Women have 12 on a side; men have 10. Men begin the game with a face (the ball is on the ground and trapped between the backs of two opposing sticks) and women begin with a draw (the ball is in the air trapped between the two sticks). Men wear helmets, gloves, shin guards and elbow pads, and body checking and stick checking are allowed; women's protective covering is restricted to shin pads only and checking is illegal.

Nonetheless, many parts of the game are similar. The object of the game is to score the most goals. Players must have at least one hand on their stick at all times, or they cannot be involved in the play. The ball can be carried down the field in the lacrosse stick, passed or kicked. The goalkeeper is allowed to touch the ball with his hands—but only to deflect it, not to catch it. There is a circle around the goal, and no attacking player is allowed inside it.

Essentially, those are the rules of lacrosse. Although the men's game is more physical, both games require stamina, endurance and an incredible amount of skill.

TOSS AND SCATTER

Number of Players: 8 or more
Equipment: stick for each player, lacrosse ball

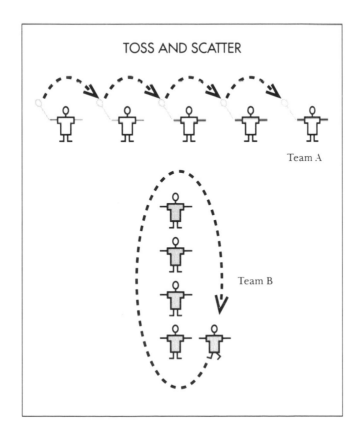

Playing Area: field
Ages: 10 and up

For Toss and Scatter, players divide into two teams, A and B, and stand together in the center of the field to start play. Team A tosses the ball into the air and then scatters to cover as much of the field as possible. Team B catches the ball. If the ball hits the ground before being caught, a player from Team B must scoop it up and toss it to a teammate, thus giving Team A more time to cover the field.

Once a Team B player safely has the ball, he whips it to any area on the field, preferably away from a Team A player. After Team B has thrown the ball, its members line up one behind the other. The tosser sprints around the line of his teammates as many times as he can, receiving a point for each circle.

Meanwhile Team A has retrieved the ball, and its members line up as well. Members must pass the ball, net to net, from the front of the line to the back. They yell "Stop!" when the ball reaches the end of the line.

Team B totals its points and the teams switch roles. The team with the most points after everyone has thrown the ball is the winner.

BLOCK OUT

Number of Players: 2 or more
Equipment: stick for each player, balls, chalk
Playing Area: wall
Ages: 10 and up

See BLOCK OUT (football).

TARGET PRACTICE

Number of Players: 2 or more
Equipment: stick and ball for each player
Playing Area: two benches with targets on them
Ages: 8 and up

Target practice is another game for developing accuracy. Players should line bowling pins or tennis ball cans on two benches and divide into two teams, one in front of each bench. The goal is to be the first team to knock over all of the cans on the bench. Distances from the shooting area and the benches can vary depending on the skill level of the participants. If there is not an unlimited supply of balls, players should split their team in half, one on either side of the bench, so less time is spent retrieving balls.

GOALIE

Number of Players: 2
Equipment: stick for each player, lacrosse ball
Playing Area: backyard with goal area marked
Ages: 8 and up

The players set up a goal in the playing area. One player, the goalie, does his best to keep the ball from going into the goal. The other player tries to get the ball past him in 10 shots (or some other number that the players agree on). He gets a point each time he succeeds. After 10, the players switch positions. The first player to reach 15 points wins.

It's a good idea to draw a boundary line to keep the shooters far enough away from the goal so the goalie doesn't get hurt by a ball coming in too fast and too close.

W A L L B A L L

Number of Players: 2
Equipment: stick for each player, lacrosse ball
Playing Area: wall
Ages: 8 and up

In Wallball, two players alternate throws, each trying to create a carom off the wall that will be difficult for the opponent to field. It might be good to draw a line on the wall to prevent a player from throwing it so low that the opponent has no chance of retrieving it. Play continues until someone misses the ball. Each ball is worth one point, and play goes to 15. If the skill level is low, one bounce might be allowed.

K N O C K - O U T

Number of Players: 3 or more
Equipment: stick for each player, lacrosse ball
Playing Area: wall
Ages: 8 and up

Knock-out is a great game for players who don't have much of a field but do have access to a wall. Players get in a line. The first player throws the ball at the wall and then runs to the end of the line. The second player gets the rebound before it hits the ground and throws it toward the wall again. Now he runs to the end of the line, and so on. If a player misses a rebound, then he is eliminated. The last person left is the winner.

S H U T T L E

Number of Players: 4 or more
Equipment: stick for each player, lacrosse ball
Playing Area: anywhere
Ages: 8 and up

See SHUTTLE (football).

S O L O   S H U T T L E

Number of Players: 6 or more
Equipment: stick for each player, lacrosse ball

Playing Area: anywhere
Ages: 8 and up

See SOLO SHUTTLE (badminton).

SIX-IN-A-ROW

Number of Players: 6 or more
Equipment: stick for each player, lacrosse ball
Playing Area: field
Ages: 10 and up

See SIX-IN-A-ROW (field hockey).

LACROSSE BASEBALL

Number of Players: 10 or more
Equipment: stick for each player, lacrosse ball
Playing Area: field with three bases and home plate marked
Ages: 10 and up

The more people playing Lacrosse Baseball, the better. Players divide into two equal teams, one that is up to "bat" and the other that is out in the field. Players need to have specific fielding positions for first, second, and third. If there are only five on each side, then the other two players should be the pitcher—who will cover home plate—and an outfielder. If there are more, then one can fill in for catcher and the rest the outfield positions.

The pitcher passes the ball to the batter. If he misses the throw, it counts as one strike. Three strikes equals one out. But if the batter catches it, he throws it out into the field—preferably away from the other players.

Once the batter throws the ball, he must run to all of the bases and home plate. There is no stopping. The fielders must retrieve the ball and pass to all of the bases and home plate—in order—before the runner completes his run.

If, for instance, the third baseman retrieves the ball, he passes it across the field to first. The first baseman may have to run out to meet the ball, but he must bring it back to the first-base area before he passes it to the second baseman, who then passes it to the third baseman, who then passes it home (usually covered by the pitcher).

If the runner makes it all the way around the bases before the ball does, then a run is scored. If the ball beats the runner, then the batting team has one out. After three outs, the teams switch sides. The team with the most runs at the end of nine innings wins.

MONKEY IN THE MIDDLE

Number of Players: 3 or more
Equipment: stick for each player, lacrosse ball
Playing Area: anywhere

LACROSSE

Ages: 8 and up

See MONKEY IN THE MIDDLE (field hockey).

THREE ON THREE ON THREE

Number of Players: 9 or 11 if you want to have two goalies
Equipment: stick for each player, lacrosse ball
Playing Area: field
Ages: 10 and up

See THREE ON THREE ON THREE (field hockey).

ONE GOAL

Number of Players: 8 or more
Equipment: stick for each player, lacrosse ball, two goal markers
Playing Area: small field with goal in the middle
Ages: 10 and up

See ONE GOAL (field hockey).

HOT POTATO

Number of Players: 4 or more
Equipment: stick for each player, lacrosse ball, timer with a buzzer
Playing Area: anywhere
Ages: 8 and up

Every kid has probably played Hot Potato at a birthday party at one time or another. But it also can be adapted into a great lacrosse game to improve speed and control.

Players stand in a circle. They set the timer and then pass the ball to one another as fast as possible. The player who is left holding the ball (or chasing after it because he missed it) when the timer goes off is eliminated. The last player remaining after all other players have been eliminated is the winner.

Instead of eliminating a player immediately, it also is possible to give a player a "P" the first time he is stuck with the ball, an "O" the second time, and so on to eventually spell P-O-T-A-T-O (or a shorter word). That way all players can stay in the game longer.

DOUBLE JEOPARDY

Number of Players: 4 or more
Equipment: stick for each player, two lacrosse balls
Playing Area: field with sidelines and center line
Ages: 8 and up

See DOUBLE JEOPARDY (field hockey).

11

SOCCER

The Game

While the exact origins of soccer are in dispute, it is clear that the game has been around for ages. A similar game called tsu-chu (kickball) was played in China in the third or fourth century B.C. England also takes credit for soccer, claiming that it started in the third century A.D. when Englishmen kicked the heads of conquered Danes through the streets.

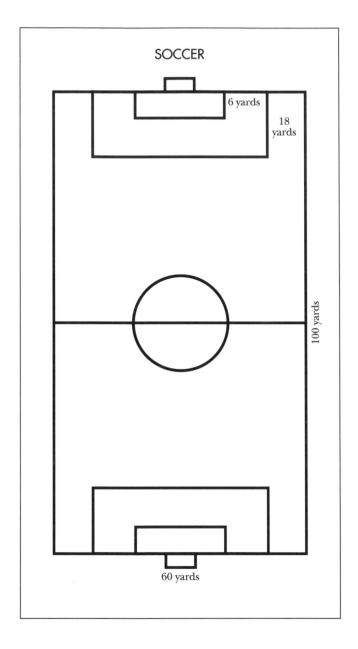

But regardless of its origins, soccer is considered by many to be the world's most popular sport, and it is very easy to play. The object of the game is to get the ball into the goal; the team that scores the most goals is the winner. The official rules decree that there should be 11 players on each team—10 field players and 1 goalkeeper—but soccer is often played pick-up style with considerably fewer than 22 players.

The kickoff begins in the center of the field, with each team lining up on its respective side. The player from the first team kicks the ball forward of the center line to another player. From that point on, this team tries to maintain control of the ball and move it toward—and eventually into—the goal. The other team's objective is to intercept the ball and move it in the opposite direction toward the other goal. Players return to the kickoff position after a goal is scored.

The game involves very few rules and restrictions. The most notable is that while a goalkeeper may touch the ball with any part of his body, the field players are not allowed to use their arms or hands. Players are allowed, however, to hit the ball with their heads (called heading) and the rest of their body.

Free kicks are awarded when players are fouled—tripped, pushed or elbowed—and when a player is offsides (if a player is closer to the opposing goal than either the ball or a defensive player) or commits a handball.

The only time a field player may touch the ball with his hands is when the ball goes out of bounds. The player must put the ball back in play by throwing it with both hands, coming straight over his head, and keeping both feet on the ground. If a ball goes over the end line, however, it is kicked in rather than thrown in.

The rules are simple in soccer and so are the skills; even a six-year-old can kick a ball. As with most sports, the challenge arises when the level of play increases. It can take years to master the intricacies of dribbling, shooting, heading and passing.

SOCCER BASEBALL

Number of Players: 10 or more
Equipment: soccer ball
Playing Area: field with three bases and home plate marked
Ages: 8 and up

The more people the better in Soccer Baseball. Players divide into two equal teams; one goes up to bat and the other plays the field. Players need to have specific fielding positions for first, second and third. If there are only five on each side, then the other two players should be the pitcher—who will cover home plate—and an outfielder. If there are more, then the other players can fill in for the catcher and the other outfield positions.

No hands are ever allowed in this game. The pitcher passes the ball to the batter with his foot. The batter kicks the ball, no matter where it is. There are no balls and strikes, but the pitcher is expected to pass the ball on the ground within the general vicinity of home plate.

Once the batter kicks the ball, he must run to all of the bases and home plate without stopping. The fielders must retrieve the ball and kick it to all of the bases and home plate, in order, before the runner completes his run.

If, for instance, the third baseman retrieves the ball, he kicks it across the field to first. The first baseman may run out to meet the ball, but he must bring it back to the first base area before he kicks it to the second baseman, who then passes it to third, who then passes it home.

If the runner makes it around the bases before the ball does, then a run is scored. If the ball beats the runner instead, then the batting team has one out.

After three outs, teams switch sides. At the end of nine innings, the team with the most runs wins.

MONKEY IN THE MIDDLE

Number of Players: 3 or more
Equipment: soccer ball
Playing Area: anywhere
Ages: 6 and up

See MONKEY IN THE MIDDLE (field hockey).

SIX-IN-A-ROW

Number of Players: 6 or more
Equipment: soccer ball
Playing Area: field
Ages: 8 and up

See SIX-IN-A-ROW (field hockey).

FOOSEBALL

Number of Players: 12 or more
Equipment: soccer ball
Playing Area: field with four zones marked
Ages: 8 and up

See FOOSEBALL (field hockey).

FOUR GOALS

Number of Players: 6 or more
Equipment: soccer ball
Playing Area: field with four goals marked
Ages: 8 and up

See FOUR GOALS (field hockey).

PARTNERS

Number of Players: 4 or more
Equipment: soccer ball
Playing Area: field with four goals marked
Ages: 8 and up

See PARTNERS (field hockey).

CORNERS

Number of Players: 4
Equipment: soccer ball

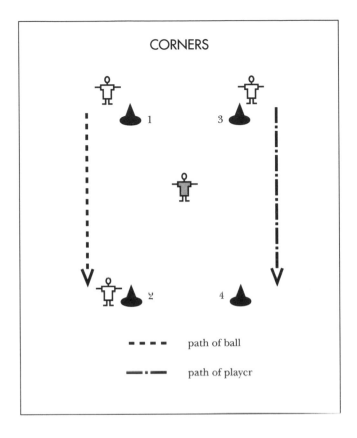

Playing Area: square with definite boundaries
Ages: 8 and up

Corners is similar to MONKEY IN THE MIDDLE, except that the outside players are limited as to where their passes can go. This makes it easier for the middle person, although it is now three against one.

The three outside people are positioned on three of the four corners of the square. The middle person stands inside the square. The outside people may pass only along the lines of the square, not across the middle. They also may move only along the lines of the square and not cut across the middle.

To facilitate passing, a player should always have two passing options, which means that the players on the outside of the square are constantly switching corners. For instance, if the ball starts in corner 1, corners 2 and 3 are adjacent and corner 4 is opposite. The other players should be in corners 2 and 3. Then if the ball is passed from corner 1 to corner 2, the player who is in corner 1 stays where he is—still adjacent to the corner with the ball—but the player from corner 3 must run over to corner 4 to provide the second passing alternative, because corner 4 is now the adjacent corner.

This game is excellent for helping players learn to move into the open position when receiving a pass. If the middle person is able to get the ball away from an outside person, then he and the outside person who made the error switch places.

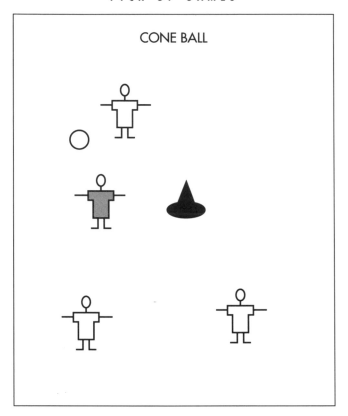

CONE BALL

C O N E   B A L L

Number of Players: 4
Equipment: soccer ball and a cone
Playing Area: small circle with cone in the center
Ages: 8 and up

Cone Ball is MONKEY IN THE MIDDLE with another variation. And like CORNERS, this game is three against one. The difference is that while the three on the outside want to keep the ball away from the person on the inside, this is not their primary goal. The object is to hit the cone in the center of the circle. The person on the inside does his best to prevent this. By passing quickly across the circle, players may be able to catch the defender on the wrong side of the cone and be able to get a shot off.

If the player on the inside gets the ball away, he exchanges places with the person he stole it from. If a player hits the cone, he gets a point and then goes into the middle to defend against other players getting a point. The player with the most points at the end of an allotted period of time is the winner.

T H R E E   O N   T H R E E   O N   T H R E E

Number of Players: 9 or 11 if you want to have two goalies
Equipment: soccer ball

Playing Area: field
Ages: 8 and up

See THREE ON THREE ON THREE (field hockey).

JUGGLING

Number of Players: 1 or more
Equipment: soccer ball for each player
Playing Area: anywhere
Ages: 8 and up

Juggling is the term used for keeping the soccer ball up in the air, without allowing it to touch the ground. Players can use any part of the body that is legal in the game of soccer, such as the knee, foot and head.

The object of this game is to juggle as many times as possible, with the players counting the number of times the ball hits the body. The player who can juggle the most times in a row is the winner.

If one player is juggling all by himself, then he can set a goal to reach and see if he can get there in a certain amount of time; or he can simply try to beat his highest number of consecutive hits.

GROUP JUGGLING

Number of Players: 3 or more
Equipment: soccer ball
Playing Area: anywhere
Ages: 8 and up

For Group Juggling, players should organize themselves into a fairly small circle. One player lightly tosses the ball to the next player in the circle. This player juggles the ball as long as he wants (it might be only one juggle), and then pops it over to the next person in the circle. This continues until the ball hits the ground. Players in the circle decide whether it was the passer or the receiver who made the mistake—that person is eliminated. The last player left juggling the ball is the winner.

ORIGIN OF HACKEYSACK

During the early 1980s, soccer-style juggling almost became a sport in its own right. A small cloth bag filled with beans called a Hackeysack was marketed with huge success. Players used soccer juggling skills to keep the Hackeysack in the air, and competition was fierce to be the player or team that could keep the ball in the air longest. The fad has died down considerably since its heyday, but there are still some avid Hackeysack players in this country.

HUNTER

Number of Players: 3 or more
Equipment: soccer ball for every player except one
Playing Area: anywhere
Ages: 8 and up

Hunter is another juggling game. All of the players except for one have a ball, and they begin juggling them. The player without the ball—known as the hunter—moves among the jugglers, distracting but not interfering with them and not using his hands. As soon as one of the jugglers loses the ball, the hunter tries to gain possession of it. If he's successful, then he begins juggling and the player who lost the ball becomes the hunter.

THROUGH THE LEGS

Number of Players: 4
Equipment: soccer ball, timer
Playing Area: anywhere
Ages: 8 and up

Through the Legs is a workout, and it really develops dribbling and ball-handling skills. Players divide into two teams. One player from each team plays the goal,

THROUGH THE LEGS

which players create by standing about 30 feet apart from each other and spreading their legs. The other two players battle it out in between.

A goal is scored when the ball goes through the opponent's legs, either forward or backward. There are no boundaries to the playing field. The players in goal may not move their legs in any manner to block the ball.

One of the goals should be holding the timer. After two minutes, the goals and the players switch. After all four players have gone three times each, the team with the highest number of goals is the winner.

GOALIE

Number of Players: 2 to 4
Equipment: soccer ball
Playing Area: wall or small area with goal marked
Ages: 6 and up

See GOALIE (lacrosse).

WALLBALL

Number of Players: 2
Equipment: soccer ball
Playing Area: wall
Ages: 6 and up

See WALLBALL (lacrosse).

KNOCK-OUT

Number of Players: 3 or more
Equipment: soccer ball
Playing Area: wall
Ages: 6 and up

See KNOCK-OUT (lacrosse).

DODGEBALL

Number of Players: 10 or more
Equipment: one or more soccer balls (also, clock or timer with buzzer for variation)
Playing Area: circle
Ages: 6 and up

Players divide into two teams. One team forms a fairly large circle, while the other takes up positions inside the circle. It's good to draw the circle physically in some way, so the boundary lines are clear.

The team on the outside has one or more soccer balls. These players must kick the balls and try to hit the players on the inside. When a player on the inside gets hit, he must leave the circle.

121

Play ends when everyone on the inside has been eliminated. A clock is used to see how long it took the team on the outside to eliminate the inside people. The two teams switch, and the other team tries to beat the time of the first team.

A variation on this is to set the amount of time beforehand—three minutes, for example. When the buzzer sounds at the end of the time period, the number of players left in the circle equal the number of points for that team. The other team then goes in for three minutes and tries to keep more players alive.

PROGRESSIVE DODGEBALL

Number of Players: 10 or more
Equipment: soccer ball for each player
Playing Area: circle
Ages: 6 and up

Like DODGEBALL, Progressive Dodgeball confines the players to a limited area. Unlike Dodgeball, there are no teams. One player begins with the ball. The rest are targets. The player with the ball does his best to kick the ball at the other players and hit them. Once he hits a player, that player gets another ball and joins the attacking player. The group that is trying to avoid getting hit becomes progressively smaller, until only one is left—that player is the winner.

TEN AND AGAIN

Number of Players: 5 or more
Equipment: soccer ball
Playing Area: anywhere
Ages: 6 and up

Ten and Again is very similar to DODGEBALL, but in this game only one player is the target and only one ball is used. The one player stands alone in the center of a circle that is formed by the other players. If he is able to survive 10 kicks without being hit, he stays in the middle and gets to do it again.

Players on the outside are allowed to pass to one another to get a better shot off, but they must first yell "pass" to distinguish the kick from one of the 10 kicks that the middle player must survive.

The person who hits the middle person is the next one to go in the center. The person who comes out of the center starts the play.

SOCCER GOLF

Number of Players: 2 or more
Equipment: soccer ball for each player
Playing Area: field with cones or markers
Ages: 6 and up

Soccer Golf is good for developing a player's accuracy. Cones or other markers should be spread around the field, a good distance apart from each other. Players "tee off" and head toward the first marker, keeping track of how many kicks it takes to get there. Once both (or all) players reach the marker, the player with the fewest strokes for that "hole" chooses which marker they go after next. When all markers have been hit, the player who has completed the course in the fewest strokes is the winner.

BULL IN THE RING

Number of Players: 3 or more
Equipment: soccer ball for each player
Playing Area: field
Ages: 6 and up

See BULL IN THE RING (basketball).

BULLS VERSUS COWS

Number of Players: 4 or more
Equipment: one soccer ball for every two players
Playing area: field
Ages: 8 and up

See BULLS VERSUS COWS (basketball).

LINE SOCCER

Number of Players: 8 or more
Equipment: soccer ball
Playing Area: field with two parallel boundary lines
Ages: 8 and up

See LINE HOCKEY (field hockey).

SQUARE SOCCER

Number of Players: 4 or more
Equipment: one or more soccer balls
Playing Area: small square (10' x 10')
Ages: 8 and up

This game has some similarities to LINE SOCCER (field hockey). Players divide into two equal teams and confine themselves to a small square. Each team is responsible for two sides of the square; the object is to kick the ball over the other team's sides.

Players stand on the edge of the square and do not go into the center. The ball pops back and forth between the teams like a ball in a pinball machine. If the ball does leave the square, then the team that is not defending the side that it crossed gets a point. The first team to reach 15 points wins. If many people are playing, more soccer balls can be added to make the game more challenging.

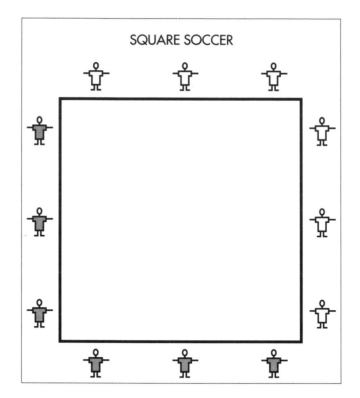

SQUARE SOCCER

O N E   G O A L

Number of Players: 8 or more
Equipment: soccer ball, two goal markers
Playing Area: small field with goal in the middle
Ages: 8 and up

See ONE GOAL (field hockey).

H O T   P O T A T O

Number of Players: 4 or more
Equipment: soccer ball, timer with buzzer
Playing Area: anywhere
Ages: 6 and up

See HOT POTATO (lacrosse).

D U C K

Number of Players: 8 or more
Equipment: soccer ball for each player
Playing Area: anywhere
Ages: 6 and up

See DUCK (basketball).

SOCCER

HANDBALL

Number of Players: 8 or more
Equipment: soccer ball
Playing Area: field
Ages: 10 and up

Handball is the one soccer game in which players can use their hands. Players divide equally into two teams. The play is the same as in regular soccer, except now a player can catch or stop the ball with his hands.

The player with the ball moves down the field, dribbling either the traditional way with his foot or basketball style with one hand. He may not move with the ball if he is not dribbling it in some manner. Passes can be either kicked or thrown.

The goalie may not come out of the penalty box, but no one else is allowed in there. At the end of a specified amount of time, the team with the most goals wins.

INDOOR SOCCER

Number of Players: 12
Equipment: soccer ball
Playing Area: indoor soccer arena
Ages: 6 and up

Indoor Soccer is a fast-paced game, usually a little more violent and often higher scoring than regular soccer. Some people predict that this is the form of soccer that will catch on in the United States, because it is much easier to follow on television than regular soccer.

The game is played with the same size ball, but the field is significantly smaller (200 ft. long and 85 feet wide, compared to 330 ft. and 180 ft. for regular soccer). Each team consists of five players and a goalkeeper. The big difference, however, is that the walls are in play. Players use the walls almost as teammates, passing the ball against them and running to receive it after it comes back at an angle.

DOUBLE JEOPARDY

Number of Players: 4 or more
Equipment: soccer ball
Playing Area: field with line in the middle
Ages: 8 and up

See DOUBLE JEOPARDY (field hockey).

12

T E N N I S

The Game

Tennis is a sport that used to belong to the elite, probably because the first courts were established at private clubs or estates. But today public courts have made this a popular sport for everyone.

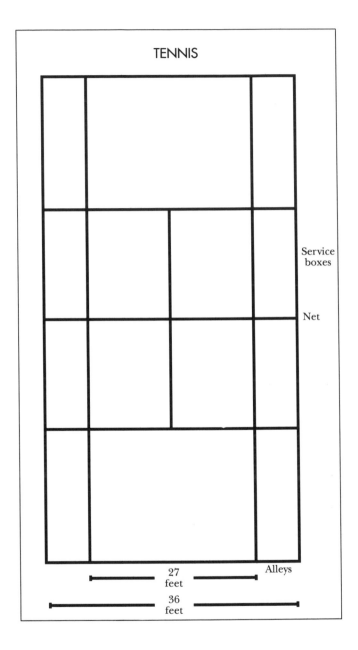

The tennis court is divided in half by a net, with one player on each side (or two on each side if it's a doubles game). Play begins with a serve from the right-hand service box. The receiver gets to the ball—allowing it to bounce only once—and returns it back to the server. Play continues in this manner until one player fails to return the ball within one bounce, safely over the net and within the bounds of the court. The other player then gets a point.

After each point, the server alternates which side of the court he serves to (that is, on the second serve, he stands on the left side of his court and serves to the opponent's left-hand service box). Servers are allowed two attempts for each serve.

Scoring is probably the most difficult part of the game. To win a match, a player needs to win two out of three sets (or three out of five in some tournaments). To win a set, a player needs to win at least six games and must win by two. To win a game, a player needs at least four points and must win by two.

The points make it even more confusing. The four points are 15, 30, 40, and game. Zero is referred to as "love." For instance, a 1–0 score in a normal game would be considered a 15–love score in tennis. If the score is tied at 40–40, that is called "deuce." The player who gets a point after deuce has the "ad" point, which means he must get the next point to win the game; otherwise the score goes back to deuce.

TWENTY-ONE

Number of Players: 2
Equipment: racket for each player, tennis ball
Playing Area: tennis court
Ages: 8 and up

The basics of Twenty-One are similar to regular tennis, but the different scoring motivates players to rush the net more often.

The game begins with a serve. For every winning shot—one that the opponent just can't get to and not an unforced error by the other player—from the baseline, the player scores one point. For every winning volley shot from the net, the player scores two points. The first player to reach 21 wins.

This encourages players to rush the net to get more points, but it also shows them how damaging it can be to do so at inappropriate times because the opponent can hit the ball out of reach.

TOP OF THE HILL

Number of Players: 4 or more
Equipment: two rackets and one tennis ball per court
Playing Area: one court for every two players
Ages: 8 and up

In Top of the Hill, the number of players determines the number of courts used. For instance, if six players are involved, then there will be three courts. Each half of each court is ranked. The highest-ranked net—sides 1 and 2—is called the "top of the hill." Players draw lots to see who starts on which court.

The higher rank serves to the lower rank, and one volley is played out. For all places except the top of the hill, the winner of the rally moves to the next court. The losers stay where they are.

The only place where the winner gets a point is at the top of the hill. The loser of this rally goes back to the lowest-ranked court. The loser of each game always serves for the next rally. The player who has collected the most points from the top of the hill at the end of a designated time is the winner.

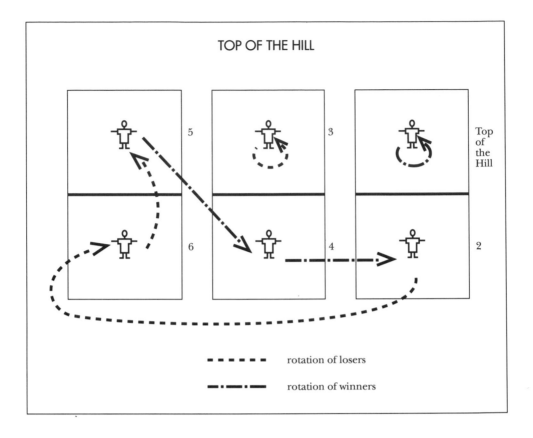

TOP OF THE HILL

rotation of losers

rotation of winners

If there are an odd number of people or too few courts for the number of players, then a line can be formed near the last ranked court. People wait in the line until it's their turn to play.

TOP OF THE HILL—DOUBLES

Number of Players: 8 or more
Equipment: racket for each player, tennis balls
Playing Area: one court for every four players
Ages: 8 and up

Top of the Hill changes slightly when it is played with doubles teams. Instead of winning one point, the players must win an entire game, unless the game at the top of the hill is over first. If so, all other games end and the winning team is the one with the most points. If a game is tied, one more point may be played.

Rotation is slightly different too. As before, the top-of-the-hill winners stay where they are and the top-of-the-hill losers go down to the lowest-ranked court; but this time they split up the team, one on each side of the net. The winners and losers of the other games also split up, unless they are about to enter the top-of-the-hill court. Otherwise rotation remains the same. The winner is the one who has won the most games after the playing time is over.

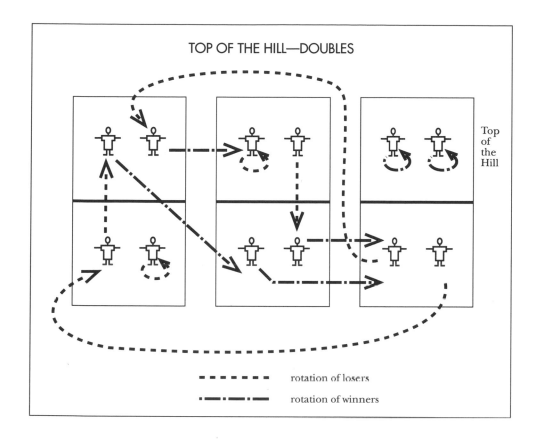

TOP OF THE HILL—DOUBLES

- - - - - rotation of losers

·—·—·—·— rotation of winners

T I N Y   T E N N I S

Number of Players: ?
Equipment: racket for each player, tennis ball
Playing Area: service box area of tennis court
Ages: 6 and up

Tiny Tennis is just like regular tennis, except the court is reduced to only the service boxes and—in the case of very small players—to only one side of the service boxes.

Play begins with a drop-ball serve (not an overhead serve). Each time the ball crosses the net, it must bounce in the service box area. Players cannot hit the ball out of the air, or it will count as a point against them. Players also lose a point if the ball they hit does not land in the service box area. Scoring is the same as in regular tennis.

O N E   O N   Y O U

Number of Players: 2
Equipment: racket for each player, tennis ball
Playing Area: tennis court
Ages: 10 and up

There is probably no better pick-up game for the beginning of the tennis season than One on You. This time is usually fraught with frustrations and pointless errors. Playing the real game of tennis turns into a serve/error/point situation, with rallies few and far between and very few chances for good winning shots. One on You can change all of this.

When players are just getting started, double faults are common, and they're not a fun way for the opponent to win the point. Therefore, in this game each player gets three serves instead of two, which also gives the rusty player more serve work. But a triple fault still results in a point for the nonserver.

Once the players get past the serve and the rallying begins, the scoring gets a little more complicated. The numbers are still 15, 30, 40, game (with deuce thrown in for a tie), but an unforced error does not count as a full point. It counts as "one on you" or "one on me," depending on who makes the unforced error. Because a full point has not been won yet, the server continues to serve from the same side.

The second unforced error by the same person is called "two on you" and the third is "three on you." When "three on you" is reached, then the person not making the errors gets a point (that is, 15, 30, 40 or game), and play resumes.

If, however, a player has one or two on him and the other player makes an unforced error, then the first player's errors are erased, and the other player now has one on him. In otherwords, a player must make three unforced errors in a row in order to lose a point.

It is possible to gain points by winners, however. For instance, if one player hits a great shot down the line that his opponent has no chance of getting, all of the "on you" points are erased, and the player gets the point immediately.

A L L E Y   R A L L Y

Number of Players: 2
Equipment: racket for each player, tennis ball
Playing Area: the alley area of a court
Ages: 10 and up

Alley Rally is one of the best control games in tennis. The rules and scoring are exactly the same as in regular tennis, but the playing area is limited to the alley only. Unlike ONE ON YOU, the points in this game rarely will come from winning shots; more likely, they will be errors when players' shots go outside the four-foot-wide alley area.

H O R S E

Number of Players: 2 or more
Equipment: racket for each player, bucket of balls
Playing Area: court
Ages: 8 and up

Horse helps a tennis player develop control with a variety of shots, yet the game also can be silly fun.

The first player announces a shot. It can be something simple, such as a serve into the left service box, or it can be something crazy, such as a lob shot into the back court while the player is on his knees. If the player successfully completes the shot he describes, then the next player must duplicate that shot exactly. If the second player is able to do so, then the first player (or the third player if there are more than two) must do the shot again. This goes on until someone misses. That person has an "H." Play continues in this manner until someone has spelled out H-O-R-S-E, and loses the game.

There is no penalty if a player misses the first shot in a series. The next player is then free to create a shot of his own.

VIC-O-RAMA

Number of Players: 8 or more
Equipment: racket for each player, tennis ball
Playing Area: one court
Ages: 8 and up

Players should divide into two teams. The first two players from each go out on the court and play out one point. After the point, the winner stays on, and one more member of his team joins him. The loser leaves the court and the next player on his team takes his place. So now it is two members of the first team playing against one member of the second team.

If the first team wins again, it adds a third member of its team to the court. Now it's those three against the third player (all alone) from the second team.

If the second team now wins, it adds a person to the court, and the three from the first team must leave the court. The next person from their team comes out to battle the two from the second team.

Whichever team has the singles player on it plays only in the single court. The other team—no matter how many players they have—plays in the doubles court. The game ends when one team has managed to win enough points in a row so that the entire team is on the court at once.

HANDBALL TENNIS

Number of Players: 2 or 4
Equipment: tennis ball
Playing Area: service boxes of tennis court
Ages: 6 and up

When players find themselves on a court without a racket, Handball Tennis is the perfect alternative. The game is the same as tennis, except only a small portion of the court is used—usually the service boxes—and hands are the main piece of equipment.

Players bat the ball back and forth with their hands. The hands must remain stiff, as catching the ball will cause a player to lose a point. Players are allowed to use both hands, although not at the same time.

THE GAME OF PAUME

Handball Tennis is less of a variation of tennis than it is a precursor. The game of paume was played in France long before tennis was invented anywhere else. The paume players used a small court with a net stretched across it. They batted the paumeball back and forth across this net with the "palms" of their hands—hence the derivation of the "paume."

○

GOALIE

Number of Players: 2 to 4
Equipment: racket for each player, tennis ball
Playing Area: backboard or court with goal area marked
Ages: 8 and up

Goalie is a great game to play against a backboard or wall. Mark off one section of the backboard as the goal. One player, the goalie, stands in front of the goal area with his racket and does his best to keep the tennis ball from going into the goal. This is great work for the volley shot.

The other player tries to serve the ball past the goalie. If he succeeds, he gets a point. If the goalie blocks it with a volley, then the other player must fire a shot in again with either a backhand or a forehand, depending on how the ball is returned to him.

If there are several players shooting at the goal, then they take different areas of the court or take turns hitting the ball. Players switch with the goalie after a specified amount of time. The player with the most goals wins.

It's a good idea to draw a boundary line (at least 8 feet) to keep the shooters back far enough away from the goal, so the goalie doesn't get hurt by a ball coming in too fast or too close.

WALLBALL

Number of Players: 2
Equipment: racket for each player, tennis ball
Playing Area: backboard
Ages: 8 and up

See WALLBALL (lacrosse).

15–30–40–GAME

Number of Players: 2
Equipment: racket for each player, tennis ball
Playing Area: backboard or wall with designated areas marked
Ages: 8 and up

TENNIS

To play 15–30–40–Game, players must first set up four targets on the backboard or wall. One should be marked 15, the next 30, the next 40, and the last GAME. One player serves to the wall. The next player gets the rebound and hits it toward the 15 target. If he gets it, that is his score and he moves on to 30; if he misses, the first player gets the rebound and also tries for the 15 target. Players must start over if they miss any of the targets; they keep rallying until one player has hit all four targets in order. The first player to do this wins the game. There are no deuce or ad points; the winner is the one who gets two out of three sets, just as in regular tennis.

If the rally dies before someone wins the game, then the player who made the bad shot is the one who serves to the wall. You cannot score on a serve.

KNOCK-OUT

Number of Players: 3 or more
Equipment: racket for each player, tennis ball
Playing Area: wall
Ages: 8 and up

See KNOCK-OUT (lacrosse).

TENNIS HOCKEY

Number of Players: 6 or more
Equipment: racket for each player, tennis ball
Playing Area: a gym or a tennis court without a net
Ages: 8 and up

This is a variation of GOALIE that can be used with larger groups. Two goals should be marked off at both ends of the gym, the way it would be in regular hockey. Players divide into two teams, and two players are chosen as goalies for their respective teams. As in Goalie, these players will have a lot of volleying work as they protect the goal.

The rest of the players take their positions on the floor. One team starts the play with a serve. Each team tries to get the ball into the opposite goal. Players may stop a ball flying by them by holding out their hand, but they may not catch the ball. Once the ball drops in front of them, they then hit it with their racket either to pass to a teammate or shoot for the goal. The team with the most goals at the end of a specified period wins.

If play gets too rough (with players wildly swinging their rackets), it is a good idea to give players their own square on the floor. They are not allowed out of the square, and they are responsible for any balls that come into it.

TENNIS VOLLEYBALL

Number of Players: 6 or more
Equipment: racket for each player, tennis ball
Playing Area: tennis court
Ages: 8 and up

135

MALAYSIAN FOOT TENNIS

In Malaysia, a game called foot tennis is popular. It's a combination of tennis and soccer because although its rules and court are closer to tennis, the ball is closer to the size of a soccer ball. One side serves the ball. It may bounce once, but then it must be returned to the other side. If a team fails to do this successfully, then the other side gets a point.   ○

The rules in this game are similar to volleyball, although it is played on a tennis court.

The net on the tennis court represents the "volleyball" net. The players divide into two equal teams. Play begins with a tennis serve, and the ball should go to the person standing in the correct service box. The receiving team has three tries to get the ball back over the net without letting it hit the ground, even on the serve.

Play continues in this manner until the ball goes out of bounds or hits the ground. If the serving team is the winner, it gets a point. If it was the receiving team, it gets the serve (and not the point). Play goes to 15.

Players may vary the rules governing the type of hits they may use. Smashes can be outlawed and all shots can be required to be lofted first, to make the rallies last a bit longer.

TENNIS BASEBALL

Number of Players: 6 or more
Equipment: two rackets, tennis ball
Playing Area: tennis court
Ages: 8 and up

The players divide into two equal teams, the batting team and the fielding team. The bases are the two net posts (first and third) and the two hashmarks at each baseline (second and home).

The fielding team spreads out on half of the court, which is called the field. Only the pitcher has to use a racket; the rest of the players may use their hands. The field is divided into three areas: the two service boxes are singles; the back-court area is a double; and the alleys are triples. The homerun does not exist in Tennis Baseball.

The batting team stands behind the baseline on the other side of the court. One player comes up to bat. The pitcher sends the ball toward the batter in any manner he prefers and at any spot on the court, as long as he uses a racket and as long as the ball stays within the bounds of the court. The batter only gets one chance.

The batter hits the ball with the racket, aiming for one of the three areas on the other side. If the ball is fielded in the air it is an out, but if it lands in one of the designated areas it is a single, double, or triple, depending on the location. The player advances that many bases, and his teammate comes up to bat. Three outs and the teams switch roles. Play goes for nine innings.

POPOVER

Number of Players: 3 or more
Equipment: racket for each player, tennis ball
Playing Area: anywhere
Ages: 8 and up

Everyone spreads out in a large circle. One player starts with the ball and bounces it off his racket up into the air to the next person in the circle. That person then must hit it to the person after him without letting the ball touch the ground.

If a person misses, then he is eliminated and must go to the center of the circle for the remainder of the game. The group decides whether it was the hitter or the receiver who made the error. The last person left is the winner.

ROTATION TENNIS

Number of Players: 8 or more
Equipment: racket for each player, tennis ball
Playing Area: tennis court
Ages: 10 and up

For Rotation Tennis, players take up positions around the perimeter of the court. They should be as evenly spaced as possible. Everyone plays for himself. The one nearest the baseline hashmark starts the play, serving to the player nearest the hashmark on the opposite court. After he serves he rotates clockwise, and the player behind him rotates into position at the baseline. The same rotation happens on the other side.

The object is then to keep the ball in play. If a player fails to do this, he is eliminated and must step outside the rotation. As more and more players get eliminated, it becomes increasingly difficult to get into position on time. Players find themselves sprinting around the court.

When it winds down to three players, a player's best bet is a lob shot, which will give him time to reach the other end of the court. When it gets down to two players, they just play out the point to find the eventual winner.

SHUTTLE

Number of Players: 4 or more
Equipment: at least two rackets, tennis ball
Playing Area: tennis court
Ages: 8 and up

See SHUTTLE (badminton).

SOLO SHUTTLE

Number of Players: 6 or more
Equipment: racket for each player, tennis ball

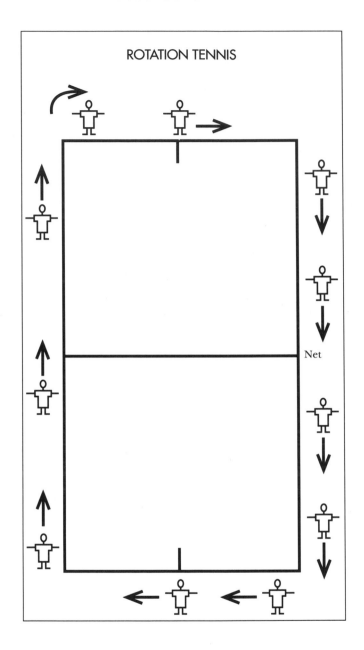

ROTATION TENNIS

Playing Area: tennis court
Ages: 8 and up

See SOLO SHUTTLE (badminton).

FIELDERBALL

Number of Players: 3 or more
Equipment: racket for each player, bucket of balls

TENNIS

Playing Area: tennis court
Ages: 8 and up

Fielderball is another game for a larger group. One player (usually a coach) is the feeder who stands near the net with a large bucket of balls. The rest of the players line up at the baseline on the other side of the net.

The feeder hits a shot to the first person in line. This player must return the ball past the feeder so that it lands within the bounds of the singles court. If he does, he goes to the end of the line.

If he misses, however, he must leave his racket at the net post and sprint around to the feeder side, where he becomes a fielder. This is when Fielderball starts to get interesting.

The next person in line has a more difficult task. Even though he can hit the ball into the doubles court, he now must return the ball past the feeder *and* the fielder. If the fielder catches the ball or if the ball goes out of bounds, the hitter becomes a fielder. Any fielder who catches a ball may pick up his racket and return to the hitting side.

Play continues until there is only one person left on the hitting side, who is declared the winner. The game also can end when all the balls are gone, which means the players left on the hitting side are the winners.

If the number of balls is running low, fielders may want to retrieve some stray ones, so they will have more chances to get back to the hitting side before the bucket empties.

TARGET

Number of Players: 2 (or additional pairs)
Equipment: two rackets, three balls, for each pair of players
Playing Area: the alley area of a tennis court
Ages: 6 and up

Target is a game for two people, but many pairs can play it at once on the same court. This game is good for practicing racket control.

Each pair of players should have three tennis balls. Two of the balls are placed opposite one another on the alley lines. One player stands behind each of these balls. The third ball is the one in play.

The game begins with a drop-hit. Players try to hit their opponent's target ball with the ball in play, but all hits must be little taps that the opponent can return. In other words, a player cannot smash the ball toward the target ball. The first player to hit the opponent's ball is the winner.

CANADIAN DOUBLES

Number of Players: 3
Equipment: racket for each player, tennis balls
Playing Area: tennis court
Ages: 8 and up

The game of tennis is ideally suited for two or four players. But what happens when there are three players?

Then the group can play what is called Canadian Doubles. One player is the singles player, and the other two are doubles players. The doubles players' side of the court includes the alleys, while the singles player's side uses just the singles court. The game is played like regular tennis, except that play must go to three sets, and each player must play an entire set as the singles player. At the end, the individual games are added up, and the player who has won the most games is the winner.

13

VOLLEYBALL

The Game

Like basketball, volleyball was invented as a YMCA winter sport. It was created by William Morgan, who called the game "mintonette." He stretched a tennis net high up over a basketball court and used the inside of a basketball as the ball. The name was changed to volleyball because the point of the game is to volley the ball back and forth across the net.

Volleyball is relatively simple. Six players on each team line up on both sides of the net. One team serves the ball to the other, and the receiving team has three hits to keep the ball off the ground and return it to the other side, with no player hitting the ball twice in a row. (In championship volleyball, players also use a move called a block, which means stopping the ball before it goes all the way over the net. The block does not count as one of the three hits.) If the ball touches the ground, is not returned or goes out of bounds on the other side, then the opposite team wins that volley.

The server must stand beyond the endline on his side of the court. The net is out of play on a serve, but during the volley, the ball can be played off the net. Only the serving team can score a point. If the nonserving team wins the volley, then it has the opportunity to be the serving team. After the nonserving team wins a point, it rotates one position before it starts serving. In this manner, the server, the net people and the back-row people are always changing. The first team to reach 15 points wins the game.

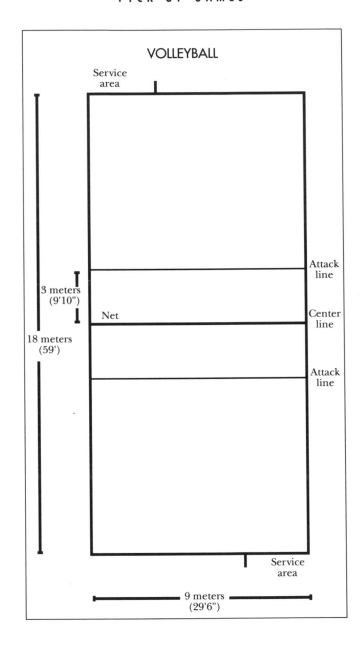

VOLLEYBALL

WALLEYBALL

Number of Players: 4 or more
Equipment: volleyball, net
Playing Area: racketball court or some enclosed area
Ages: 8 and up

Walleyball doesn't have too many rules that are different from normal volleyball. The primary difference is the location—it is played in a racketball court or some other similar enclosed area. The net stretches from one wall to the other and all walls are in play.

In one sense, this is an easier game than volleyball, because there is no out of bounds; but in another sense, there are some very different skills involved. Players have to react to the angle of the ball coming straight over the net. Also, the back walls are in play, and it's especially difficult to field the ball after a low back-wall hit.

BEACH VOLLEYBALL

Number of Players: 4
Equipment: volleyball, net
Playing Area: beach
Ages: 8 and up

Thousands of people have set up volleyball nets on the beach and have played Beach Volleyball, but there is also an official version of the game.

The game is played with four people, two on each side. Games are still played 15 points, just as in regular volleyball, but players switch sides after a total of five points.

There are still three hits to a side, but the block definitely counts as one of the three hits. In this game, however, the blocker can play the second ball. But the biggest difference is the fact that the players are outside in soft sand—wind and sun really come into play. The wind blows the ball, and the sun gets in players' eyes. In fact, the sun can actually be part of a player's strategy; he can hit a high lob right where his opponents can't see it. Even when they do find it, they'll be slightly blinded from having stared at the sun.

TOP OF THE HILL

Number of Players: 8 or more
Equipment: volleyball and net for each group of four
Playing Area: beach
Ages: 8 and up

If there are large numbers of BEACH VOLLEYBALL players, Top of the Hill can be a great way to get them mingling and playing on different teams against different people.

The number of players determines the number of nets used. For instance, if six players are involved, then there will be three nets. Each net is ranked, the highest being called the "top of the hill." Players draw lots to see who starts on which court.

The games go to five, and it's not necessary to win by two. The winners on the top-of-the-hill court stay where they are, and they each get a point; this is the only place where players win points. Also, players should keep track of their own points because they will not necessarily stay together as a team.

The top-of-the-hill losers go to the lowest-ranked net and split up, one on each side of the net. The winners of the other games move up in rank and also split up, unless they are entering the top-of-the-hill court. The losers of the other games also split up, but they remain on the same court.

WALL SERVE

Number of Players: 4 or more
Equipment: volleyball
Playing Area: wall with line on it 10 feet high
Ages: 6 and up

Wall Serve is the perfect game for beginners and players who are trying to develop a new serve. Players divide into two teams. The first player in each line is behind the service line. The second player runs up in order to be halfway between him and the wall. The other team is set up the same way.

When play starts, the server serves to the wall. The serve must be over the line, and the second person must go out to catch the rebound. If this happens, the team gets a point. The second player then takes the ball back behind the line to serve, while the third player goes out to retrieve the ball. The first team to reach 15 points wins.

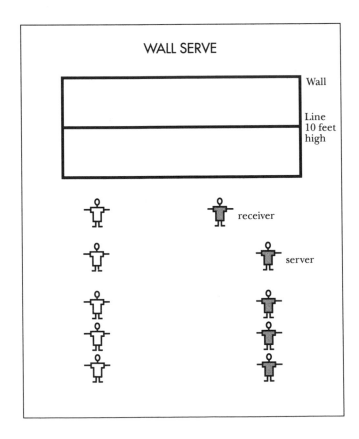

TARGET SERVE

Number of Players: 2 or more
Equipment: volleyball, net, targets
Playing Area: volleyball court
Ages: 10 and up

Target Serve is a serving game for more advanced players. Players divide into two equal teams, one on each side of the net. A target, such as a cone or a chair, is set up on each side in the same place. The placement of the target depends on what the players are trying to work on: line serves, cross-court serves, deep serves, short serves, and the like.

Players alternate serving across the court toward the target. If the target is hit, then that team scores one point. If the ball hits the net or goes out of bounds, then one point is subtracted. No points are given or subtracted for a good serve that does not hit the target. The first team to reach 15 points wins.

NAMEBALL

Number of Players: 3 or more
Equipment: volleyball
Playing Area: anywhere
Ages: 6 and up

Setting the ball—a controlled two handed hit to another player—is one of the most important skills a volleyball player can learn, and Nameball is a good place for a beginning player to start. Another nice thing about it is that it is not essential to have a net.

Players stand in a fairly large circle. One player tosses the ball up into the middle of the circle and calls out the name of someone else there. That person must go into the circle, set the ball up again and call out someone else's name. The balls set up should be hit straight up into the center of the circle and not to a person.

This game can be played without scoring or, if players want to score, then they can give points for each miss of a set, whether by setter or receiver. After a certain amount of time has elapsed, the player with the fewest points wins.

SETTER'S CHALLENGE

Number of Players: 1 or more
Equipment: volleyball
Playing Area: anywhere
Ages: 10 and up

Setter's Challenge is another setting game, but it is for more advanced players. In this game, a person sets to himself, but all sets must be at least 10 feet high and must be performed in a specific sequence.

Each group of sets is done four times, with six sets total. First the player does four overhand sets. Next he does four underhanded sets. Then he alternates overhand and underhand. Then he sets, turns in a circle and sets again. Fifth, he sets, touches one knee to the floor and then sets again. And finally, he sets, sits down, stands up and sets again.

If a player is by himself, he should count how many attempts he needs before he can do the entire sequence without making a mistake. He must start over from the beginning each time.

If two or more players are challenging each other, the rules change slightly. Only one ball is used and players take turns. The first player to do the entire sequence is the winner. If a player misses one of his sets, he hands the ball to the next person. His next time up, he goes back to the beginning of the sequence.

A player does have an alternative option, however. After the fourth set in a group, he may call "I'm stopping" and hand the ball to the next player. When the ball comes around to him next, he can pick up from where he left off. It is important that he calls this only at the end of a group of four.

SET BASKETBALL

Number of Players: 2 or more
Equipment: volleyball
Playing Area: basketball net
Ages: 10 and up

This game is used to improve setting accuracy. The object is to set the ball into the basketball net. Play starts with one person at the foul line, who sets the ball toward the basket. If it goes in, he gets a point. If it comes off on a rebound, another player calls for it and sets it back up. If the rebound is unplayable, then another player goes to the foul line and play starts from there again. The first player to reach 15 points is the winner.

POPCORN

Number of Players: 4 or more
Equipment: volleyball for each group of two or three
Playing Area: anywhere
Ages: 8 and up

This is another excellent game to play when there isn't a net. It works well with larger groups. Players divide into pairs or triples, depending on what works best with the number of people available. Each group should have a ball, and the players should be spread a good distance apart from one another.

One player sets the ball to his partner, who then sends it back again. The object of the game is to be the team that pops the ball back and forth to each other the longest, without the ball hitting the ground.

If the skill level of the players is high, then this game can be done on the run, forcing the players to move to a new spot on the floor each time they receive the ball.

BALLOON VOLLEYBALL

Number of Players: 2 or more
Equipment: balloon or beach ball, net
Playing Area: volleyball court
Ages: 6 and up

This game is just like volleyball, except that a balloon or beach ball is used instead of a volleyball and a few restrictions can be changed to make it more interesting. It's a good idea to increase the number of hits per side. Also, depending on the age of the players, hitting the ball twice in a row can now be made legal.

SHUTTLE

Number of Players: 4 or more
Equipment: volleyball, net
Playing Area: volleyball court
Ages: 8 and up

See SHUTTLE (football).

SOLO SHUTTLE

Number of Players: 6 or more
Equipment: volleyball, net
Playing Area: volleyball court
Ages: 8 and up

See SOLO SHUTTLE (badminton).

NEWCOMB

Number of Players: 4 or more
Equipment: volleyball, net
Playing Area: volleyball court
Ages: 5 and up

Newcomb is volleyball for beginners. It allows small children to get the idea of volleyball before they have acquired enough skills to truly play it.

Players toss the ball back and forth over the net. They must catch it, without allowing it to touch the ground. They may throw it to a teammate, but they may not move with the ball. If the ball does hit the ground, then the other team gets a point. The first team to get 15 points is the winner.

FISTBALL

Number of Players: 4 or more
Equipment: volleyball, net
Playing Area: volleyball court
Ages: 6 and up

This game falls somewhere between regular volleyball and NEWCOMB. It's great for younger players who don't quite have the skills needed for traditional volleyball.

The object of the game—to be the first to reach 15 points—is the same. Points are scored when the opposing team misses the ball, hits it out, hits it into the net or lets the ball bounce more than once for each hit.

One of the major differences between this game and the others is that the ball is allowed one bounce before a player hits it. Also, any number of players on a team may hit the ball before they send it back over the net. The final requirement is that all balls must be hit with the fist.

CROSSCOURT

Number of Players: 8 or more
Equipment: volleyball
Playing Area: four nets put together in the shape of a cross
Ages: 10 and up

While Crosscourt can be played with as few as eight players, the more people the better. Players divide into four equal teams and set up in each of the courts created by the four nets. The nets should all have one center pole in common and radiate out at right angles from that.

One team begins with a serve to any of the other three courts. The players on that court then hit the ball to any other court, with the rules being identical to regular volleyball. The differences arise in the scoring, and the fact that four

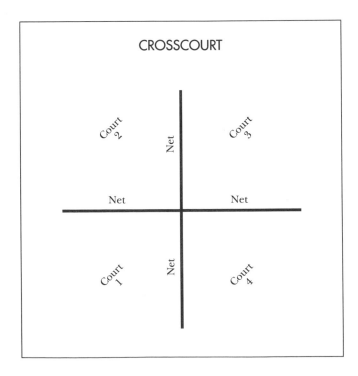

CROSSCOURT

148

teams are playing rather than two. In this game, points are negative. When one team reaches 15 points, it has lost, and the game is over. The team with the fewest points is the winner.

Points are given when the ball touches the ground, is hit out of bounds or isn't sent to a new court within three hits of the ball. After a point is scored, the serve rotates clockwise to the next court.

To make this game more difficult, a second or even third ball can be added. This is not a good idea if there are only a few players; but with large groups, it makes it much more fun.

14

WATER SPORTS

The Game

Because the term "water sports" encompasses so much, it is difficult to say that the games are all variations of one original sport. It is also hard to give a general estimate as to when and where water sports began, but it's a good bet that water sports—especially racing—have been around since humans discovered water and its unique properties.

RACING

Number of Players: 2 or more
Equipment: none
Playing Area: pool
Ages: 5 and up

There is probably nothing simpler than a race, yet it still can provide more fun than many other games. The type and length of the race can vary—it can be backstroke, breaststroke, no arms, underwater or some combination. People can do it individually or in relays. With a little imagination, the possibilities are endless.

WATER POLO

Number of Players: 14 plus a referee
Equipment: water polo ball
Playing Area: pool with a goal at either end
Ages: 10 and up

151

The object of Water Polo is to score more goals than the opposing team. There are seven players to a side in the official game, although it can easily be played with less.

To start, players line up touching their end of the pool. A referee blows a whistle and tosses the ball into the center. The players swim out to try to get it. After that, they try to pass to teammates, dribble (place the ball in the water in front of them and swim, pushing it with the head and body) and shoot on goal. The team with the most goals after a specified period of time wins.

The ball cannot be held underwater or punched. A player is not allowed to splash water in his opponent's face, kick, strike, hold, pull someone back or get in the way of an opponent (unless he has the ball).

With the exception of the goalie, players are not allowed to touch the ball with both hands at once, and no one is allowed to touch the sides or the bottom of the pool. These restrictions make Water Polo grueling, but it's also a lot of fun.

MARCO POLO

Number of Players: 2 or more
Equipment: none
Playing Area: pool
Ages: 5 and up

The main idea of Marco Polo is that one player is "blind." (He closes his eyes.) It is his job to tag another player who can see, at which point they trade places. It sounds fairly difficult, but the blind player may yell "Marco" whenever he wishes. All of the other players must respond by yelling "Polo" back to him. No one is allowed to put his head underwater, because everyone must be able to hear and respond at all times.

BUOYBALL

Number of Players: 4 or more
Equipment: tennis ball, life buoy (life preserver)
Playing Area: pool
Ages: 10 and up

Buoyball is one of the more exciting yet complicated water sports. Players divide into two teams, one on each end of the pool. The object of Buoyball is to toss—not dunk—the tennis ball into the buoy (floating life preserver) located in the center of the pool. Players are not allowed to swim while the tennis ball is in their hands; therefore, they must either shoot at the buoy or pass it to a teammate who is closer to the buoy. Players without the ball are allowed to swim anywhere they please.

Each buoyball (when the ball goes through the buoy), counts as a point. The team with the most points at the end of a set period of time is the winner.

After a buoyball is scored, both teams must swim back and touch their end of the pool. All players on one team must remain at their edge of the pool until the entire team touches it.

After a buoyball, possession goes to the team who did not score, and it is that team's responsibility to retrieve the tennis ball. This is the only time that players may touch the buoy. They may move it back to the center if they wish, because it probably will have shifted due to the wave motion. If the buoy is in an advantageous position, however, they may choose not to move it. If a player touches the buoy during play, then the other team gets a free shot from its end zone.

SHARK

Number of Players: 3 or more
Equipment: none
Playing Area: pool
Ages: 6 and up

One player is designated as the "shark." The rest of the people are fish. The fish must swim across the pool and back without getting tagged by the shark. The starting end of the pool is the only safety zone. Once a fish is tagged by the shark, he becomes a shark as well. The winner of the game is the last fish left.

There is, however, one big hitch. The sharks must at all times put one hand on their hips—with their elbow sticking up—to imitate the fin of a shark. That leaves them only one hand to swim with, while the fish have use of both hands.

SHUTTLE

Number of Players: 4 or more
Equipment: beach ball, rope or net
Playing Area: pool
Ages: 8 and up

See SHUTTLE (football).

DOLPHINS AND MINNOWS

Number of Players: 4 or more
Equipment: none
Playing Area: pool
Ages: 6 and up

Dolphins and Minnows is a game that is fairly similar to SHARK. In this case, the players are divided into two teams, the dolphins and the minnows. The minnows must get from one end of the pool to the other without getting tagged by the dolphins. Underwater is a safe zone, where a minnow cannot be tagged.

The tagged minnows go to the edge of the pool as soon as they are tagged. The safe minnows keep on swimming toward the end of the pool. If a minnow makes it to the end without getting tagged, then he scores a point for his team. The minnow team counts up the number of points it has, and then its players become the dolphins. After each team has had a chance to be a minnow, the game is over. The team with the most points wins.

VARMINT BALL

Number of Players: 4 or more
Equipment: beach ball
Playing Area: pool with two goals
Ages: 10 and up

Varmint Ball is a cross between MARCO POLO and football, and should be played only by people who are prepared to get physical. There are two goals, one at each end of the pool. The players divide into two teams, each defending its own goal.

The object of the game is to get the beach ball in the goal. However, a player may never hold the beach ball in his hand; instead, if he would like to "carry" it, he must tap it gently in the air above his fingertips as he swims toward the goal.

The football aspect comes into it because the other team may "tackle" the person with the ball at any time. This rule ensures that people won't do much traveling with the ball anyway. It's much more efficient to pass it to a teammate. The team with the most goals wins.

WATER VOLLEYBALL

Number of Players: 4 or more
Equipment: volleyball or beach ball, net

154

Playing Area: pool
Ages: 8 and up

Water Volleyball is the game of volleyball played in a pool. Three hits are allowed per side, and the ball must not touch the water. If players are using a small pool with a shallow end and a deep end, they may chose not to allow the shallow-end players to stand on the floor. As this is difficult to prevent, it might be better to give the deep-end people an extra hit or reduce their playing area in proportion to balance out the game.

JUMP/DIVE

Number of Players: 2 or more
Equipment: none
Playing Area: pool, diving board (preferable)
Ages: 6 and up

Jump/Dive can result in a number of painful bellyflops, but that's almost the point of the game. One player stands on the diving board. The other player is on the edge of the pool. As the player on the diving board bounces high in the air off the board, the player on the edge shouts out "jump" or "dive." The player who has gone off the board must then do his best to enter the water feet first if it's a jump, or headfirst if it's a dive. Players get a point for each successful completion; the player with the most points at the end wins.

The player on the edge shouldn't call until the diver's feet have left the board; but he must do it on the diver's way up, and not as he's starting to come down. It is perfectly acceptable for the caller to observe what the diver is anticipating and then call the opposite.

WATER BASKETBALL

Number of Players: 2 or more
Equipment: ball and floating hoops or the equivalent
Playing Area: pool
Ages: 8 and up

For two to four players of Water Basketball, participants might want to use only one hoop (as in HALFCOURT basketball) and have each team bring the ball back past a certain line to start play. For larger groups, it's better to have a basket at each end of the pool.

The object of the game is to get the ball in the basket and score a point. The first team to reach 21 wins. Players may not touch other players and, depending on their swimming skills, may not touch the bottom of the pool.

If a player has possession of the ball, he may shoot, pass or dribble. Dribbling consists of putting the ball in the water in front of him and swimming while protecting it with the arms and body. No player is allowed to carry the ball and swim at the same time.

155

DIVING FOR PENNIES

Number of Players: 2 or more
Equipment: many pennies
Playing Area: pool
Ages: 6 and up

Diving for Pennies is a treasure hunt that most young children love, and it's very simple to play. A collection of pennies is thrown into the pool. The minute they hit the water, all of the players jump into the pool after them and try to grab as many as possible. The player who collects the most pennies is the winner.

If only a few pennies are used, the game can be varied to keep it interesting. One player jumps in at a time; his goal is to collect as many pennies as possible before they hit the bottom of the pool. All of the pennies are then retrieved and it's the next person's turn. The player who gets the most is the winner.

15

M O R E   F U N
A N D   G A M E S

None of the games in this chapter evolved from any particular sport. Some may be combinations of sports; others may be games in their own right. No matter what their origins, however, all of them are a lot of fun to play.

TAG

Number of Players: 2 or more
Equipment: none
Playing Area: anywhere
Ages: 4 and up

Tag is one of the simplest games ever invented. One person is designated "It." That person must then tag another person in order to escape the "It" label. The person who is tagged becomes the new "It." The people who are not "It" do their best to escape by running away. There is no end to this game, and therefore no winner or loser.

BALL TAG

Number of Players: 3 or more
Equipment: ball (or beanbag) for each player
Playing Area: anywhere
Ages: 4 and up

There are a number of ways to make TAG more interesting, and one of them is Ball Tag. In this game, all players carry a ball (or beanbag), and as before, one player begins as "It." Instead of tagging the other players with his hand, he must hit them with his ball, preferably below the shoulders. Once a player has been hit, he joins "It" and uses his ball to try to hit the remaining players. "It" hits players for the entire game, with other "Its" joining him, until all but one person is eliminated. That person is the winner. The first person who was tagged by "It" becomes the new "It" for the second round.

FREEZE TAG

Number of Players: 4 or more
Equipment: none
Playing Area: anywhere
Ages: 4 and up

Freeze Tag is the same as TAG, except it is played by two even teams. One team is "It." Whenever its members tag a member of the other team, that person must stand absolutely still—in other words, freeze. The team that is "It" must freeze all of the players on the other team. A player can unfreeze a teammate by tagging him. A variation of this game, which makes unfreezing a little more difficult, requires a player to crawl through his teammate's legs in order to unfreeze him.

CAPTURE THE FLAG

Number of Players: 6 or more
Equipment: two flags
Playing Area: anywhere
Ages: 8 and up

Capture the Flag is basically a very elaborate form of FREEZE TAG. Players divide into two equal teams. Each team has its own flag to protect, and the object of the game is to steal the opponent's flag.

Each team controls half of the playing area, which is either marked by a center line or designated beforehand in some manner. In this area, the team locates its flag and designates a "prison."

If an opponent crosses into a team's area, he can be tagged. If he is tagged, he is sent to the prison area, where he must remain until one of his own teammates tags him.

If a player captures an opponent's flag, he must bring it back to his area in order for his team to win. If he is tagged on his way back, then he is sent to prison, but the flag remains in the new position.

The game can be played on a regular playing field, but if there is a large number of people, it's best to play it in a much larger area. For example, a neighborhood can be divided up, one block for each team or one side of the street against the other side, with the street as a neutral zone. Some camps play the game using the entire camp. If the game is played on this scale, then just locating the flag takes considerable effort.

STEAL THE BACON

Number of Players: 8 or more (plus a referee)
Equipment: bowling pin
Playing Area: anywhere
Ages: 6 and up

For this game, players divide into two teams and form lines facing each other. Directly in the center of the playing area is a bowling pin—or a similar object that stands upright—known as the bacon.

Players on both teams are assigned numbers, one through however many people are participating. When the referee calls out a number at random, the player with that number from each team must run to the center and try to "steal the bacon." If the player makes it back to his side with the bacon, he receives a point. However, the player from the other team can chase his opponent with the bacon to his line and tag him to receive a point for his team.

Sometimes players are faced with a stand-off in the center; both try to fake each other out and steal the bacon, but neither wants to risk taking it and getting tagged. The referee then has the option of sending those players back and calling new numbers, or leaving the two players in and calling additional numbers. If there are more than eight people playing, referees can call out two, three or even all numbers from the onset.

The winning team is the one that has the most total points after a given amount of time.

KICK THE CAN

Number of Players: 3 or more
Equipment: can or plastic bottle
Playing Area: anywhere
Ages: 6 and up

Kick the Can is basically hide-and-go-seek with a few variations. One spot is designated as a prison, while another location is set as the spot for the can. One unfortunate player (usually the loser in HOT POTATO or the last person to call "Not It") must search and tag all of the other players, who are in hiding.

But the searcher (or "It") has one major handicap: He cannot go out too far because he must protect the can from being kicked by the players who are hiding. If one of the hiding players kicks the can, the searcher must retrieve it and put it back in its rightful position before he can tag someone. The hiding players may kick the can as many times as they like, as long as they can avoid being tagged.

The goal of the seeker is to find and tag all hiders and place them in prison in order to end the round. (If six or more people are playing, it is a good idea to make two people seekers or divide into teams, as one person might be "It" for hours.) When he is finally able to tag everyone, a new game begins and the first person he tagged becomes "It."

EARTHBALL

Number of Players: 6 or more
Equipment: earthball
Playing Area: field with two endlines
Ages: 8 and up

It would be hard to find an Earthball game these days, but it was very popular back in the early part of the 20th century. The earthball itself is the reason that the game lost its popularity. As it's about six feet high, an earthball isn't exactly something that the average person can store in his garage. It's also very heavy.

To play Earthball, players divide into two equal teams. The earthball is placed in the center of the field. The object is for one team to push the earthball over the opponent's endline. That's all there is to it—it's sort of a tug of war in reverse—but it's "enormously" entertaining.

BOCCE BALL

Number of Players: 2 or more
Equipment: bocce ball set
Playing Area: anywhere
Ages: 8 and up

A bocce ball set consists of two different-colored sets of four balls and one smaller target ball. Players divide into two equal teams.

One player tosses the target ball anywhere he pleases, near or far. The object is to then get more of the team balls close to this target ball than any of the other team's balls.

Teams alternate throws. A player's throw may knock the other team's balls out of the way, and it may also knock the target ball into a more (or less) advantageous position. After all eight balls are thrown, players move to the target ball and see whose balls are closest.

Only one team can score at each turn. If Team A has one ball closer than any of Team B's balls, Team A gets one point. If it has two balls closer than any of Team B's balls, Team A gets two points, and so on. The first team to reach 15 points wins.

HORSESHOES

Number of Players: 2 or 4
Equipment: horseshoes, stakes
Playing Area: lawn
Ages: 6 and up

For this game, two stakes are driven into the ground, a good throwing distance apart from each other (30 to 40 feet). Play begins at one of the sticks. One player tosses his horseshoes one at a time, at the other stake. Then the other player does the same.

The object of the game is to toss the horseshoes around the stake; a horseshoe around the stake is known as a ringer, which is worth three points. If there is no ringer, then the horseshoe closest to the stake gets one point. If a player has both of his horseshoes closer to the stake than his opponent's horseshoes, then the player gets two points. The first player to reach 50 points wins.

HOPSCOTCH

Number of Players: 2 or 3
Equipment: pebble or coin, chalk

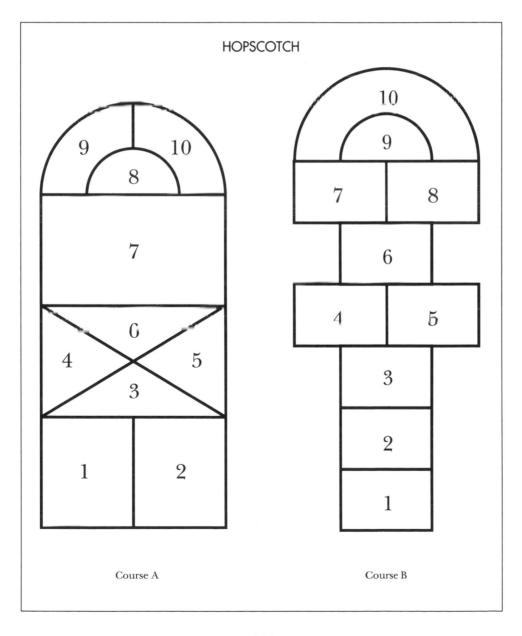

HOPSCOTCH

Course A   Course B

Playing Area: hopscotch course
Ages: 5 and up

The design of Hopscotch (also known as Potsy) varies from playground to playground, but the rules are the same no matter what the course looks like. A course is generally divided into 10 numbered boxes. All play begins at the end closest to box number one.

The first player tosses his pebble into the first box. If the pebble lands in the box, the player then hops through the course, placing only one foot in each box and being careful not to step on any lines. The player must avoid stepping in the box that contains his or any other player's pebble. At the end of the course, the player turns around and hops back. When he reaches the box with his pebble, he must bend over and pick it up and then hop off the course. If he is successful, he pitches the pebble to the next consecutive box. Play goes on in this manner until the player makes an error, either in hopping or pitching.

When a player is not successful in his hop through the course, he leaves his pebble in the box that he was trying to complete. If a player is not successful in pitching the pebble, he may place it in the intended box, but his turn is over.

While hopping, a player may land on both feet—one in each box—if two boxes are parallel to each other and the starting line and as long as there is no pebble in one of the boxes. For example, in Course A (see diagram) it would be boxes 1 and 2, 4 and 5, and 9 and 10; in Course B it would be boxes 4 and 5 and boxes 7 and 8. For all of the other boxes, the player may hop on one foot only.

The player who makes it through the course first is the winner.

JUMPROPE

Number of Players: 1 or more
Equipment: jumprope
Playing Area: anywhere
Ages: 5 and up

A game of Jumprope can be found in progress at almost any playground at a given time. The idea is for a person to swing a rope around in a circle and successfully jump it as many times as possible. If there are two players, then one end of the rope may be tied to something (a tree, for example), or players can each hold one end and jump at the same time. For three or more people, two players swing the rope and one jumps; the game becomes even more fun as the jumpers perform a wide variety of maneuvers.

If there is an even larger number of jumpers, then a game called "Follow the Leader" can be played, in which the first player entering the rope performs some action and then leaves. Every player after him must do the same; players are eliminated when they cannot.

Frequently, rhymes are made up to sing along with the jumping and to remind the jumper of the action he is supposed to perform. In addition to regular jumping, the actions might include speed jumping (where the rope is twirled faster), touching the ground, jumping on one foot, turning around or entering and exiting while the rope is spinning.

MANHUNT

Number of Players: 8 or more (the more the better)
Equipment: none
Playing Area: street with boundaries
Ages: 8 and up

Manhunt is a team version of hide-and-go-seek that is best played in a neighborhood with a lot of kids and many good hiding spots.

Players divide into two even teams and set up their own respective "prisons." One team starts out as the "hunters," while the other is the "hunted." During an allotted period of time, the team being hunted finds spots to hide within the established boundaries; the hunters then try to find and tag them. Once players are tagged, they must go to their opponent's prison and wait to be rescued by a teammate (by a tag) or until it's their turn to become the hunters.

After a certain amount of time, the prisoners are freed and teams switch roles. The team that gets the most prisoners after both sides have been the hunters is the winner.

PING PONG

Number of Players: 2 or 4
Equipment: paddle for each player, Ping Pong ball
Playing Area: Ping Pong table
Ages: 8 and up

Ping Pong is also called Table Tennis because, essentially, it is a game of tennis played on a table.

The table is divided in half by a low net. Each half of the table is bisected by a line.

Play begins with one player serving to the other. The serve must bounce once on the server's side and once on the opponent's side in the box diagonal to the server's box. A player serves five times and then the serve switches to the opponent. The game goes to 21 points, but a player must win by two.

Points are scored whenever an opponent is unable to return the ball successfully, because he missed it, hit it into the net, hit it off the table or allowed it to bounce more than once before he hit it. Only on the serve is a player allowed—and, in fact, required—to let the ball bounce once on his own side.

During a doubles game, play gets a little more complicated. Teammates must alternate hits, regardless of where the ball is hit. For the serve, however, one player alone serves his block of five.

RED ROVER

Number of Players: 4 and up
Equipment: none
Playing Area: anywhere outdoors
Ages: 6 and up

This is a fun, albeit somewhat aggressive, game for younger groups. Players form two equal teams and face each other. Teammates hold each other's hands tightly and as units march toward the other team to break through the line. As teams collide, the players chant: "Red rover, red rover, send _____ over," calling the name of the player they intend to prevent from breaking through their line and bring to their side.

Players must be offensive and defensive at the same time: They have to try to get through the line, guard against being taken by the other side and help try to take the called-out player from the other side. Once players are taken and become part of the opposite team, they shouldn't forget which team they started on, because they can be stolen back by their teammates.

This crazy game frequently gets muddled amid the general confusion of switching sides; for this reason there really are no winners and losers.

TETHERBALL

Number of Players: 2
Equipment: tetherball
Playing Area: tetherball area
Ages: 6 and up

Tetherball is a unique and vigorous game for two people. The tetherball court consists of a tall pole (about 10 feet high) with a rope attached at the top. On the other end of the rope is the ball, which is essentially a volleyball. A line is painted about four feet down from the top. The pole is located in the center of a circle, and the circle is bisected by a line, designating each player's half.

The object of the game is to wind the ball and the entire length of the rope around the pole above the line. One player begins the game with any of the volleyball serves. The other player must remain on his side and bat the ball back around in the opposite direction. Players may use one hand or both hands to hit the ball, but they may not catch the ball.

If the rope starts to wind below the painted line, then it is the other player's serve. The player who manages to wind the rope entirely in his direction is the winner.

TENNIS TETHERBALL

Number of Players: 2
Equipment: racket for each player, tennis ball on a tetherball pole
Playing Area: tetherball court
Ages: 6 and up

If a tennis ball is suspended from a tetherball rope instead of the traditional volleyball, then a new game is created, which can help tennis players hone their skills.

The rules are the same as in regular TETHERBALL, except that players use rackets instead of their hands to hit the ball.

Appendix A:
PICK-UP GAMES BY NUMBER OF PLAYERS

PICK-UP GAME/BASE SPORT	NUMBER OF PLAYERS							
	1	2	3	4	5+	6+	8+	More
Alley Rally/Tennis		*						
Angel Devil/Golf		*						
Animal Ball/Football			*	*				
Around the World								
Basketball		*	*	*				
Football		*	*	*				
Association Football/Football			*	*	*	*		
Attack/Field Hockey	*	*						
Balloon Volleyball/Volleyball	*	*	*	*	*	*		
Balloonminton/Badminton	*			*				
Ball Tag/More Fun and Games		*	*	*	*	*	*	
Beach Volleyball/Volleyball				*				
Best Ball/Golf				*				
Block Out								
Football	*	*	*					
Lacrosse	*	*	*					
Bocce Ball/More Fun and Games	*	*	*					
Bolf/Basketball	*	*	*					
Boxball/Baseball	*							

PICK-UP GAMES

PICK-UP GAME/BASE SPORT	NUMBER OF PLAYERS							
	1	2	3	4	5+	6+	8+	More
British Croquet/Croquet		*	*					
Broomball/Ice Hockey						*	*	
Bulletball/Football							*	*
Bull in the Ring								
Basketball			*	*	*	*	*	
Field Hockey			*	*	*	*	*	
Soccer			*	*	*	*	*	
Bulls Versus Cows								
Basketball				*	*	*	*	
Field Hockey				*	*	*	*	
Soccer				*	*	*	*	
Bunk Baseball/Baseball	*	*	*					
Buntball/Baseball							*	*
Buoyball/Water Sports				*	*	*	*	
Call It First/Baseball					*	*	*	
Canadian Doubles/Tennis			*					
Captain and Crew/Golf								*
Capture the Flag/More Fun and Games						*	*	*
Circle Frisbee/Frisbee			*	*				
Completion/Football				*	*	*	*	
Cone Ball/Soccer				*				
Corners								
Basketball				*				
Soccer				*				
Crosscourt/Volleyball							*	*
Defender/Golf			*					
Derby Ball/Baseball				*				
Diving for Pennies/Water Sports	*	*	*	*	*	*	*	*
Dodgeball/Soccer								*
Dolphins and Minnows/Water Sports				*	*	*	*	
Double Disc/Frisbee				*				
Double Jeopardy								
Field Hockey				*	*	*	*	
Ice Hockey				*	*	*	*	

APPENDIX A

PICK-UP GAME/BASE SPORT	NUMBER OF PLAYERS							
	1	2	3	4	5+	6+	8+	More
Lacrosse				*	*	*	*	
Soccer				*	*	*	*	
Doubles/Baseball		*	*	*				
Dribble and Drive/Field Hockey						*	*	
Driving Range Target/Golf		*						
Duck								
Basketball							*	
Ice Hockey							*	
Soccer							*	
Earthball/More Fun and Games						*	*	*
Fenceball/Baseball		*	*	*	*	*	*	
Fielderball/Tennis			*	*	*	*	*	
Field Hockey Golf/Field Hockey		*	*	*	*	*	*	
15-30-40-Game/Tennis		*						
500/Baseball			*	*	*	*	*	
Fistball/Volleyball				*	*	*		
Flag Football/Football								*
Flog/Golf		*	*	*	*	*	*	
Fooseball								
Field Hockey								*
Ice Hockey								*
Soccer								*
Foot Golf/Golf		*	*					
Four Goals								
Field Hockey						*		
Ice Hockey						*		
Soccer						*		
Fours/Football				*	*	*	*	
Free for All/Field Hockey								*
Freethrows/Basketball		*						
Freeze Tag/More Fun and Games				*	*	*	*	*
Frisbee Baseball/Frisbee							*	
Frisbee Golf/Frisbee		*	*	*				
Frisbee Tennis/Frisbee		*						

PICK-UP GAME/BASE SPORT	NUMBER OF PLAYERS							
	1	2	3	4	5+	6+	8+	More
Ghostball/Basketball	*							
Goalie								
Lacrosse		*						
Soccer		*	*	*				
Tennis		*	*	*				
Golf Croquet/Croquet		*	*	*	*	*		
Group Juggling/Soccer			*	*	*	*	*	
Guts/Frisbee		*	*	*	*	*	*	
Halfcourt/Basketball		*		*		*		
Handball/Soccer							*	
Handball Tennis/Tennis		*		*				
Hockey Baseball/Field Hockey							*	
Homerun/Basketball		*						
Home Run Derby/Baseball		*	*	*				
Hopscotch/More Fun and Games		*	*					
Horse								
Baseball		*	*					
Basketball		*	*	*				
Tennis		*	*	*				
Horseshoe Golf/Golf		*	*	*	*	*	*	
Horseshoes/More Fun and Games		*		*				
Hot Potato								
Lacrosse				*	*	*	*	
Soccer				*	*	*	*	
Hotshot/Basketball		*						
Hunter/Soccer			*	*	*	*	*	
Icing/Ice Hockey		*	*	*	*	*	*	
Indoor Soccer/Soccer								*
International Croquet/Croquet		*	*	*	*	*		
Juggling/Soccer	*	*	*	*	*	*	*	*
Jump/Dive/Water Sports		*	*	*	*			
Jumprope/More Fun and Games	*	*	*	*				
Keep Away/Football			*	*	*	*		
Keep It Up/Badminton	*	*	*	*	*	*	*	

PICK-UP GAME/BASE SPORT	NUMBER OF PLAYERS							
	1	2	3	4	5+	6+	8+	More
Kickball/Baseball							*	
Kicker Golf/Football		*	*	*				
Kick Return/Football		*	*	*	*	*	*	
Kick the Can/More Fun and Games			*	*	*	*	*	*
Knockout								
Lacrosse			*	*	*	*	*	
Soccer			*	*	*	*	*	
Tennis			*	*	*	*	*	
Lacrosse Baseball/Lacrosse								*
Lay In, Stay In/Basketball		*	*	*	*	*	*	
Line Hockey								
Field Hockey							*	
Ice Hockey							*	
Line Soccer/Soccer							*	
Line-Up/Baseball						*	*	*
Make It, Take It/Basketball		*		*		*		
Manhunt/More Fun and Games							*	*
Marco Polo/Water Sports		*	*	*	*	*	*	
Match Play Golf/Golf		*	*	*	*	*	*	
Miniature Golf/Golf		*	*	*	*	*	*	
Modified Team Croquet/Croquet	*	*						
Money in the Middle								
Basketball			*					
Field Hockey			*	*	*	*	*	
Lacrosse			*	*	*	*	*	
Soccer			*	*	*	*	*	
Mushball/Basketball		*	*	*	*	*	*	
Nameball/Volleyball			*	*	*	*	*	
Newcomb/Volleyball				*	*	*	*	
One a Cat/Baseball			*	*	*	*	*	
One Goal								
Field Hockey							*	
Ice Hockey							*	
Lacrosse							*	

PICK-UP GAME/BASE SPORT	NUMBER OF PLAYERS							
	1	2	3	4	5+	6+	8+	More
Soccer							*	
One on You/Tennis		*						
Partners								
Field Hockey				*	*	*	*	
Soccer				*	*	*	*	
Pass Pattern/Football			*					
Pass Return/Football	*	*	*	*	*		*	
Pepper/Baseball				*	*	*	*	
Perimeter Hockey/Field Hockey							*	
Pickle/Baseball			*					
Pinball/Baseball			*	*	*	*		
Ping Pong/More Fun and Games		*		*				
Pinshot/Ice Hockey				*	*	*	*	
Poison/Croquet		*	*	*	*	*		
Popcorn								
Badminton			*	*	*	*	*	
Volleyball				*	*	*	*	
Popover/Tennis			*	*	*	*	*	
Progressive Dodgeball/Soccer								*
Punchball/Baseball				*	*	*	*	*
Quarterback Golf/Football	*	*	*					
Quarterback Toss/Football	*	*	*					
Racing/Water Sports	*	*	*	*	*		*	
Red Rover/More Fun and Games				*	*	*	*	
Relayminton/Badminton				*				
Rollball								
Baseball		*	*	*	*	*	*	
Football	*							
Rotation Tennis/Tennis							*	
Sandie/Golf			*					
Scoop/Field Hockey						*	*	
Scrub Ball/Baseball						*		
Set Basketball/Volleyball		*	*	*	*	*	*	
Setter's Challenge/Volleyball	*	*	*	*	*	*	*	

PICK UP GAME/BASE SPORT	NUMBER OF PLAYERS							
	1	2	3	4	5+	6+	8+	More
Shark/Water Sports			*	*	*	*	*	
Shoelaces/Baseball						*	*	
Shoot and Rebound/Basketball			*	*	*	*		
Shuttle								
Badminton						*	*	
Football			*	*	*	*	*	
Frisbee			*	*	*	*	*	
Lacrosse			*	*	*	*	*	
Tennis			*	*	*	*	*	
Volleyball			*	*	*	*	*	
Water Sports			*	*	*	*	*	
Six-in-a-Row								
Field Hockey						*	*	
Ice Hockey						*	*	
Lacrosse						*	*	
Soccer						*	*	
Sixty Second Shot/Basketball			*					
Slapshot/Ice Hockey		*						
Smear/Football			*	*	*	*	*	
Snowball/Baseball						*	*	
Snow Football/Football				*	*	*	*	
Soccer Baseball/Soccer								*
Soccer Golf/Soccer		*	*	*				
Softball/Baseball								*
Solo Shuttle								
Badminton						*	*	
Football						*	*	
Frisbee						*	*	
Lacrosse						*	*	
Tennis						*	*	
Volleyball						*	*	
Solo Volley/Badminton	*							
Speed Golf/Golf		*	*	*	*	*	*	
Speedshot/Basketball		*	*	*	*	*	*	

PICK-UP GAME/BASE SPORT	NUMBER OF PLAYERS							
	1	2	3	4	5+	6+	8+	More
Square Soccer/Soccer			*	*	*	*		
Squirrels/Basketball						*	*	
Steal the Bacon/More Fun and Games							*	*
Stepball/Baseball		*		*				
Stickball/Baseball		*	*	*	*	*	*	
Stoolball/Baseball		*	*	*	*	*	*	
Stoop/Baseball	*							
Stoopball/Baseball				*	*	*	*	
Stoop for Two/Baseball		*						
Street Hockey/Ice Hockey						*	*	
Superbounder/Basketball		*						
Superman/Basketball		*						
Tag		*	*	*	*	*	*	*
Target								
Baseball		*	*	*	*	*	*	
Basketball		*						
Tennis		*						
Target for One/Baseball	*							
Target Practice/Lacrosse		*	*	*	*	*	*	
Target Rush/Football		*	*	*	*	*	*	
Target Serve/Volleyball		*	*	*	*	*	*	
Team Croquet/Croquet				*		*		
Team Golf Croquet/Croquet		*	*	*	*	*		
Team Pinball/Baseball							*	
Ten and Again/Soccer					*			
Tennis Baseball/Tennis						*	*	
Tennis Hockey/Tennis						*	*	
Tennis Tetherball/More Fun and Games		*						
Tennis Volleyball/Tennis						*	*	
Tetherball/More Fun and Games		*						
Three Flies Up/Baseball			*	*	*	*	*	
Three on Goal/Ice Hockey			*	*	*	*	*	
Three on Three on Three								

APPENDIX A

PICK-UP GAME/BASE SPORT	NUMBER OF PLAYERS							
	1	2	3	4	5+	6+	8+	More
Field Hockey								*
Ice Hockey								*
Lacrosse								*
Soccer								*
Three Team Ball/Baseball						*		
Through the Legs/Soccer				*				
Tiny Tennis/Tennis		*						
Top of the Hill								
Badminton				*	*	*	*	
Basketball							*	
Tennis				*	*	*	*	
Volleyball							*	
Top of the Hill—Doubles								
Badminton							*	
Tennis							*	
Toss and Catch/Frisbee	*							
Toss and Scatter/Lacrosse							*	
Touch Football/Football								*
Transition Ball/Basketball								*
Triangle Ball/Baseball				*	*	*	*	
Twenty-one								
Basketball		*	*	*				
Tennis		*						
Ultimate Frisbee/Frisbee				*	*	*	*	
Universe/Basketball		*	*	*				
Varmint Ball/Water Sports				*	*	*	*	
Vic-O-Rama/Tennis							*	
Wallball								
Lacrosse		*						
Soccer		*						
Tennis		*						
Walleyball/Volleyball				*	*	*	*	
Wall Serve/Volleyball				*	*	*	*	
Water Basketball/Water Sports		*	*	*	*	*	*	

PICK-UP GAMES

PICK-UP GAME/BASE SPORT	NUMBER OF PLAYERS							
	1	2	3	4	5+	6+	8+	More
Water Polo/Water Sports								*
Water Volleyball/Water Sports			*	*	*	*		
Wiffleball/Baseball		*	*	*	*	*	*	
Wild Wickets/Croquet		*	*	*	*	*		

Appendix B:
GLOSSARY

Note to reader: Only the general sports are listed in parentheses following the entry head, not the pick-up game. If no sport is listed, the term is used in a number of sports.

A
---

ad point (tennis)   The first of two consecutive points needed after a game has reached deuce.

alley (tennis)   The area between the sidelines of a singles court and the sidelines of a doubles court.

arnie (golf)   When a player gets to the green without ever having his ball land on the fairway.

B
---

backboard (basketball)   The piece of fiberglass, metal, or wood located directly behind the basket.

ball (baseball)   A pitch that is not in the strike zone over home plate, between the knees and shoulders.

baseline (tennis)   The end line of a court.

batter (baseball)   The player who receives the pitch and attempts to hit it.

bird (badminton)   The object in play during a badminton game, usually a cork with feathers or a plastic simulation. Also called a shuttlecock.

birdie (golf)   The name given to a score that is one stroke under par for a given hole.

block   When an opponent is prevented from getting a good shot.

bounce pass (basketball)   When a player directs the ball to the floor first before it goes to a teammate. Used most often to get around the defense's arms.

box and one (basketball) A form of defense in which four players play zone defense in the form of a square while one player plays man-to-man against the best opponent.

bunt (baseball) To push the bat forward and tap the ball lightly instead of swinging.

C

---

catcher (baseball) The player who squats behind homeplate to receive the pitch.

center line The line dividing many playing areas in half.

checking To block a player's progress.

chip (golf) A short shot that lofts the ball onto the green.

conversion pass (football) A successful attempt to get two points after a touchdown instead of kicking for one.

cricket A ball and bat game, similar to baseball, that is played primarily in England.

croquet (croquet) Driving an opponent's ball away by striking one's own ball placed against it.

D

---

dead (croquet) The state of a ball after a player has hit it; a dead ball can't be hit again by a player until he has gone through a wicket.

deuce (tennis) The name for a tie score, after the teams have each won three points and until one team wins two in a row.

double (baseball) A hit that enables a player to reach second base safely in one turn.

doubles (tennis) The game in which two players are on each side of the net.

down (football) An unsuccessful attempt to move the ball 10 yards.

draw (lacrosse) The method of beginning a lacrosse game, in which the ball is trapped between two players' sticks to start.

dribbling The method used in several sports to move the ball across the playing field.

drop-ball serve (tennis) A method of putting the ball into play in which a player lets it bounce once on the court before hitting it.

E

---

endlines The boundaries marking the length of a playing area.

end zone (football) The area at either end of a football field between the goal post and the endline.

error (baseball) Any misplayed ball by a fielder.

F

---

face off (ice hockey) A method of putting the puck in play by dropping it in between two opposing players.

fairway (golf)   The mowed part of a golf course between the tee and the green.

fielder (baseball)   A player on the defensive team; the term usually is not used in reference to the pitcher or catcher.

field goal (football)   A three-point kick through the goal posts.

fly ball (baseball)   A ball that is lofted into the air as it leaves the bat.

forwards   The players on a team whose position brings them closest to the goal or basket.

foul   An infringement of the rules.

foul line (basketball)   A line 15 feet away from the basket, marking the top of the key and the place where a fouled player is given a free shot.

free throw (basketball)   The shot given to a player who has been fouled.

free-throw line (basketball)   See foul line.

G

game (tennis)   The accumulation of at least four points, the last two consecutive.

ghost runner (baseball)   An imaginary placeholder when there aren't enough players to bat and remain on the bases in the appropriate positions.

goalkeeper   The person who stands in front of the goal and attempts to block the shots at the goal. Also called goaltender or goalie.

green (golf)   The close-cut grassy area at the end of the fairway, where the hole is located.

greenie (golf)   When a player gets to the green on one stroke and yet still pars the hole.

grounder (baseball)   A ball that bounces on the ground after leaving the bat.

H

halfcourt (basketball)   When play is confined to the area on one side of the center line.

handball (soccer)   Touching a ball that is in play with the hand, arm or shoulder by anyone other than the goalie.

hashmark (tennis)   The small painted line dividing the baseline of a tennis court in half.

high sticks (field hockey)   The illegal move of raising the stick to levels where it may endanger another player.

home plate (baseball)   One corner of the baseball diamond, where a player bats and ends up after circling the bases.

homerun (baseball)   A hit that allows a player to successfully circle all of the bases and return to home plate in one turn.

I

icing (ice hockey)   Shooting a puck from the defensive end of the ice across the opponents' goal line.

infield (baseball)   The area between the bases and home plate.

inning (baseball)   A division of a baseball game in which each team gets up to bat.

interception (football) The act of catching a ball that is meant for the opponent.

J
---

juggling (soccer) The process of keeping the ball in the air using feet, thighs and the head.

jump ball (basketball) A method of putting the basketball into play at the beginning of the game, where a referee tosses the ball in the air and two opposing players attempt to bat it to their teammates.

jump shot (basketball) The method of shooting in which a player jumps into the air and releases the ball at the height of the jump.

K
---

key (basketball) A rectangular area, extending 15 feet between the basket and the foul line, where offensive players may remain no more than three consecutive seconds.

kickoff The method of putting the ball into play at the beginning, or after a point is scored, in football or soccer.

kolven A Dutch game similar to golf.

L
---

lay up (basketball) A shot made near the basket, using the backboard.

line drive (baseball) A ball that comes straight off the bat and does not loft into the air or hit the ground.

line of scrimmage (football) A horizontal line that cuts across the field at the point where the ball was last downed, behind which all players from each side must remain until the ball is snapped.

lob A lofted ball.

love (tennis) A zero score.

M
---

mallet (croquet) The implement used for striking the ball.

man-to-man A form of defense in which each player stays with an opposing player as he moves about.

match (tennis) The accumulation of sets, usually two out of three, needed to win.

mintonette The original name for volleyball.

O
---

offsides Illegally in advance of the ball or the puck.

out (baseball) An unsuccessful attempt to bat the ball and get to a base safely. A team is limited to three of these per inning.

outfield (baseball) The area beyond the bases.

out of bounds When a player or a ball goes beyond the limits of the playing area.

P

palle malle   An early French game similar to croquet.

par (golf)   The standard score for a particular hole.

penalty box (soccer)   The area in front of the goal, in which a goalie is allowed to use his hands.

pitcher (baseball)   The player who delivers the ball to the batter.

poona   A game invented in India that was very similar to badminton.

puck (ice hockey)   A flat, circular disc used instead of a ball.

punt (football)   A kick from a player's hand, usually used on the fourth down.

putt (golf)   A light tap of the ball, usually reserved for the green.

Q

quarterback (football)   The offensive player who lines up behind the center, receives the snap and usually calls the plays.

R

rally (tennis)   A series of consecutive good shots before a point is won.

rebound (basketball)   The act of taking possession of the ball after a missed shot.

referee   The official who presides over a game to make sure that the rules are followed.

rounders   A game, originating in England, similar to baseball.

rugby   A game, originating in England, similar to football.

run (baseball)   The unit of scoring in baseball, which occurs after a player has successfully touched all bases and returned to home plate.

rusher (football)   The player who tries to tackle the quarterback.

S

safety (football)   A situation when a member of the offensive team is tackled behind his own goal line.

sandie (golf)   When a player's ball lands in the sand trap, yet he is still able to make par.

serve   The method of putting the ball into play.

service box (tennis)   One of four sections on a tennis court, located next to the net, where the serve is required to bounce.

set (tennis)   A division of a tennis match that requires one player to win at least six games.

shortstop (baseball)   The position located in the infield between second base and third base.

shuttlecock (badminton)   See "bird."

sidelines   The horizontal limits of a playing area.

single (baseball)   A hit allowing the batter to reach first base successfully.

slapshot (ice hockey)   A strong shot on goal.

spaldeen   The name of the ball used in stickball.

strike (baseball)   A pitch going over the plate and passing between the batter's knees and shoulders.

T

tackle (football)   The act of forcibly bringing a player to the ground.

tee (golf)   The start of each hole, located at the beginning of the fairway.

tee off (golf)   To begin a hole.

touchdown (football)   A successful attempt to move the ball over the goal line, by running or passing. It's worth six points.

triple (baseball)   A hit allowing the batter to reach third base safely in one turn.

tsu-chu   A game, originating in China, that is similar to soccer.

U

umpire (baseball)   The official who presides over a game to make sure the rules are followed. Also calls balls and strikes.

unforced error (tennis)   A mistake or loss of a point that was not due to an opponent's good shot.

V

volley (tennis)   A quick return at the net before the ball bounces.

W

walk (baseball)   When a batter receives four balls and is allowed to take first base.

wicket (croquet)   Wire bent in the shape of an arch or rectangle that the ball must pass through.

wing   A player whose position brings him closest to the sidelines.

woodie (golf)   When a player hits a tree and still makes par on the hole.

Z

zone defense (basketball)   A form of defense in which the players guard an area on the court instead of guarding an opponent.

SUGGESTED READING

For more information on the sports described in this book, the following volumes are suggested.

Antonacci, Robert J., and Barbara D. Lockhart. *Tennis for Young Champions* (New York: McGraw-Hill, 1982).

Bulman, George. *Volleyball* (England: Ward Lock, 1989).

Charlton, James, and William Thompson. *Croquet: Its History, Strategy, Rules, and Records* (Lexington, MA: Stephen Greene Press, 1988).

James, Stuart. *Lacrosse for Beginners* (New York: Julian Messner, 1981).

John, Jenny. *Field Hockey Handbook* (Vancouver, BC, Canada: Hancock House Publishers, 1988).

Kreutzer, Peter, and Ted Kerley. *Little League's Official How-to-Play Baseball Book* (New York: Doubleday, 1990).

Olney, Ross R. *Tricky Discs: Frisbee Saucer Flying* (New York: Lothrop, Lee, and Shepard Co., 1979).

Pelton, Barry C. *Badminton* (Englewood Cliffs, NJ: Prentice-Hall, 1971).

Schellscheidt, Manny, with Deborah Wickenden. *Youth League Soccer Skills: Mastering the Ball* (Palm Beach, FL: The Athletic Institute, 1989).

Sullivan, George. *All About Football* (New York: Dodd, Mead, & Co., 1987).

Watson, Tom, with Frank Hannigan. *The Rules of Golf* (New York: Times Books, Random House, 1979).

NOTES/PHOTO CREDITS

[1] *Guinness Book of World Records.* Bantam Books, New York, 1989.
[2] Hoffman, Frank W. and Bailey, William G., *Sports & Recreational Fads.* The Haworth Press, New York, 1991.
[3] Botermans, Jack; Burrett, Tony; Van Delft, Pieter; and Van Splunteren, Carla, *The World of Games.* Facts On File, New York, 1991.

All black-and-white photos are credited to Mountain Lion, Inc., except the following:

Tennis—United States Tennis Association, p. 127
Basketball, Ice hockey and Lacrosse—Lawrence French, pp. 32, 98, 105
Frisbee—Karl Cook/Ultimate Players Association, p. 86

INDEX

Numbers in *italics* indicate a photo or illustration.